Praise for ART HEALING . . .

"Symbols are the universal form of communication. We are told even God speaks through symbols in dreams and visions. I know from my experience how insightful artwork can be for the artist and those who view his or her creative, insightful work. The unconscious can speak through our dreams and symbolic images. I find this book to be an excellent resource in understanding the process and helping us to utilize the wisdom of art in the healing process."

—Bernie Siegel, MD
Author of *Faith, Hope & Healing* and *365 Prescriptions for the Soul*

"*Art Healing* offers a refreshing and novel way to participate with art as a path to profound healing. The approach will transform the way you interact with art."

—Christiane Northrup, MD
Author of the *New York Times* bestsellers
Women's Bodies, Women's Wisdom and *The Wisdom of Menopause*

"The transformative and healing power of art is one of medicine's best-kept secrets. In this captivating book, Dr. Jeremy Spiegel shows why, using compelling, real-life examples."

—Larry Dossey, MD
Author of *The Science of Premonitions, Healing Words,*
and *Reinventing Medicine*

"Dr. Spiegel presents a true understanding of how we interact with beauty in all its manifestations. It is a must-read for scientists of the heart/mind."

—Armand DiMele
Host of "The Positive Mind with Armand DiMele," WBAI-NY
and founder of The DiMele Center for Psychotherapy, New York

"The emotional, startling, and sometimes revelatory power of art has been described by writers in the past, most notably Stendhal. The Stendhal Syndrome: 'a psychosomatic illness that causes rapid heartbeat, dizziness, fainting, confusion, and even hallucinations when an individual is exposed to art, usually when the art is particularly beautiful or a large amount of art is in a single place.'

"In *Art Healing,* Jeremy Spiegel takes this to a much higher level of understanding and clinical usefulness. He describes an exciting new technique to help people unearth the memories, feelings. and unconscious organizing principles that can hamper and sometimes cripple us. In vignettes of patients and descriptions of his own reactions to art, he describes the intrapsychic processes that are stimulated by viewing artworks, and how they lead to insights and emotional growth. He also suggests to the reader ways to use this technique in working with patients, and in viewing art oneself.

"I enthusiastically recommend this book not only to every therapist but also to anyone interested in enhancing his or her appreciation of art and understanding how it can to lead to greater emotional maturity and well-being. This book will change the way you experience art!"

—Barry M. Panter, MD
Founder and director of The American Institute of Medical Education
Fellow, American Psychiatric Association

"My interview with Jeremy is definitely one of my favorites, with his passion so evident for art healing as a path of healing."

—Lynn Thompson
Host and producer of "Living on Purpose" Radio
www.livingonpurpose.com

arthealing

VISUAL ART FOR EMOTIONAL INSIGHT
AND WELL-BEING

Jeremy Spiegel, MD

FOREWORD BY PATRICK RYOICHI NAGATANI

精神

SEISHIN
BOOKS

Portland, Maine

Published by: Seishin Books
208 Vaughan Street
Portland, ME 04102
www.thearthealing.com

Editors: Ann Mason and Ellen Kleiner
Book and cover design: Ann Lowe
Cover artwork: Nick Cave

The information in this book is designed to provide a novel, creative angle for viewing art. It is not meant to be used, nor should it be used, to diagnose or treat any medical or psychiatric condition. For diagnosis or treatment of any medical or psychiatric condition, consult your physician. The publisher and author are not responsible for any specific health, medical, or psychiatric problem that may require medical supervision and are not liable for any damages or negative consequences from any treatment or application to any person following the information in this book.

Printed and bound in the United States of America

PUBLISHER'S CATALOGING-IN-PUBLICATION DATA

Spiegel, Jeremy.

    Art healing: visual art for emotional insight and well-being / Jeremy Spiegel. Portland, Me. : Seishin Books, c2011

      p. ;cm.

      ISBN: 978-0-615-46715-3
      Includes bibliographical references.

      1. Psychotherapy. 2. Art appreciation--Psychological aspects. 3. Self-knowledge in art. 4. Art--Psychological aspects. 5. Self-perception. 6. Self-actualization (Psychology) I. Title.

BF697 .S65 2011   2011904686
158.1--dc22   1109

1 3 5 7 9 10 8 6 4 2

TO THE ARTISTS,
WITHOUT WHOSE ILLUMINATING VISION
WE'D ALL BE STUMBLING AROUND IN DARKNESS

acknowledgments

I would like to thank everyone involved, especially the artists and gallery personnel who generously provided permission to reproduce their work within these pages. I am especially indebted to Patrick Nagatani; Kenny Scharf, Mark Markin, and Paul Kasmin Gallery; Gabriel Martinez, Camilo Alvarez, and Samsøn; Lori Nix, Ellen Miller, and Miller Block Gallery; Marc Greenwold, Sandra Paci, and DC Moore Gallery; Nick Cave, Peter Haffner, Elisabeth Sann, and Jack Shainman Gallery; Marina Abramovic, Cecile Panzieri, Jessica Ventura, and Sean Kelly Gallery; Maurizio Cattelan, Catherine Belloy, and Marian Goodman Gallery; Marc Trujillo; Ling-Wen Tsai; Yeshe Parks and Whitney Art Works; Nicolas Clauss; Kelly Jo Shows, Ted Julian Arnold, and Susan Maasch Fine Art; Fabien Giraud, Raphaël Siboni, Joanne Lefrak, Anne Wrinkle, and SITE Santa Fe; Cornelia Parker, Toby Kress, and Frith Street Gallery; Shelby Spaulding, Janet Moore, and the Institute of Contemporary Art, Boston; Cheim and Read Gallery; M. Ho.

Others were integral to the development and execution of the book. Thank you to Ann Lowe, Ann Mason, and especially Ellen Kleiner, whose tireless genius and enthusiasm made this book and *The Mindful Medical Student* possible. Also, Avery Hurt tightened up an early draft of the manuscript.

Peggy Keller, Bernie Siegel, Christiane Northrup, Larry Dossey, Armand DiMele, Lynn Thompson, Barry Panter, Florian Birkmayer, Adam Stern, Ruth Gerson, Jasmine Alinder, and Janine Melillo lent expertise and support. I also thank my patients who helped me put these ideas into practice and my parents for their encouragement.

Finally, I am deeply grateful to Maya, Jonah, Summer, and Sarah for loving me.

contents

arthealing

Patrick Ryoichi Nagatani, "Yakushi Nyorai" ("The Healer")

foreword

HAVE BEEN AN ARTIST FOR OVER FORTY YEARS AND A PROFESSOR OF ART IN HIGHER education for much of my life. For twenty years, I taught photography at the University of New Mexico, guiding future artists in understanding the artworks of others and in creating their own art. Many of the ideas in Jeremy Spiegel's *Art Healing: Visual Art for Emotional Insight and Well-Being* would have been good to use for discussions in my classroom because they involve the potential for the audience's experience of self-discovery through art and because they go beyond the topics of historical concepts, categories, and analysis typically used in teaching art.

Art Healing offers numerous new and alternative insights to consider when viewing art and therapy. The book has made me think more profoundly about the viewer's perspective and experience with my artwork in comparison with my own considerations as artist, first conceptualizing then determining the aesthetic presentation of my works.

Moreover, Dr. Spiegel's definition of "art healing" has become, for me, the basis of a more serious way of looking at art. *Art Healing's* potential as a tool for self-realization, emotional healing, personality improvement, and a positive and grounded stance toward life provides an additional overlay to my thinking about art.

Recently when I visited the Philadelphia Museum of Art my openness to the ideas in *Art Healing* gave me new ways of viewing and responding to the works of Picasso, Caravaggio, and Duchamp. By focusing more on my personal interactions with the works rather than considering them in the context of art criticism or art history, I had a very insightful experience. This is the basis of *Art Healing*.

Currently, I make "tape-estries," which essentially involves painting with masking tape. I make these images through taping meditation and a desire to create images of beauty—works that Dr. Spiegel recently saw when he visited me at my studio in Albuquerque, New Mexico. While I am not a professional psychologist, I am interested in expanding awareness and personal insight. I have found that many of my readings in Buddhist philosophy correspond with ideas presented in *Art Healing*, including the promotion of openness as a state that increases the capacity for problem solving, unlocks more elusive thoughts and feelings, and helps eliminate psychological defenses that would otherwise maintain emotional stagnation.

For professionals in the field of psychology, *Art Healing* can encourage and guide "patients" to investigate artworks in which they have no past interest or even those considered ugly or unpleasant, leading them into the labyrinth of emotions as a beginning to the work of revealing and healing old wounds and conflicts.

Today, I view and talk about art in a broader way because of *Art Healing*. Thank you, Dr. Spiegel.

–Patrick Ryoichi Nagatani

preface

ART HEALING—A VISUAL ARTS-BASED TOOL FOR SELF-HEALING—IS A METHOD I devised over a period of years due to my own personal experiences interacting with many kinds of art, as well as from observations of such interactions by patients, some of whom were artists. Throughout decades of encountering art in galleries, museums, sculpture parks, black-box video installations, and avant-garde films, I have used art as a means for psychological insight and emotional healing, first unwittingly then more consciously. Viewing art gradually became less a casual pastime and more an experience of deep communion with the themes, materials, and structures of artworks. Art gave me insights into myself unmatched by anything I had gleaned from years of psychotherapy, as useful as those often painful sessions may have been.

Initially, I had no name for what I was doing but knew that on a fundamental level something positive was happening to me—that for me, participating with art could catalyze emotional healing. To my delight, I then discovered that interacting with art can reduce anxiety, minimize compulsive behavior, and lead to personal revelations that assist in overcoming self-defeating behavior patterns, positively working the clay of personality. I came to the conclusion that art could have a composite function of temple, playground, and therapist's couch. Realizing how interacting with art helped me personally over the years prompted me to teach others about my method and its potential for psychotherapeutic insights, increased personal awareness, and self-healing.

Art Healing: Visual Art for Emotional Insight and Well-Being, the culmination of this pursuit, introduces ways to optimize the power of interactions with art. The book is not a guide to appreciating art in a general sense, nor does it double as a buyer's guide for contemporary art. Rather, it illustrates a process of finding and interacting with artworks to better understand personal core issues, paving the way for transformation and healing. And since there are so many kinds of art, art healing has a variety of functions, all with the potential to provide healing benefits for people of any age and background. The healing benefits we receive from art healing depend not on our knowledge of art history, our ability to assess the value of artworks, or our capacity to place them in a cultural context but simply on our openness to them and our willingness to be led by them into our inner selves to gain insights about our core issues and how to transform negative aspects of ourselves.

Many of the ideas in this book took shape during my own interactions at various times, initially as a student and later as both psychiatrist and art lover. Over time I learned that the type of interaction with art most helpful for healing seemed to be a childlike unguarded curiosity and spontaneous merging. This insight was first inspired when, as an undergraduate at Princeton, I observed a class of preschoolers viewing an artwork outside the Department of Art and Archaeology. Seated on the grass, the children were looking at a large cement sculpture of Picasso's *Head of a Woman* with classic cubist features—asymmetrical eyes and sharp planes comprising the sides of a highly abstract face. I was fascinated by the children's responses to their teacher's question "What do you see?" One boy said, "I see eyes." Another shouted, "It looks like a sad bird!" A young girl responded, "It's weird. Kinda scary." A boy wearing overalls offered, "I think it looks like my Nana."

I felt there was something good and potentially beneficial about the children's spontaneous experiences with this artwork, in contrast to my experiences with art in classes focused on erudite analyses, historical contexts, and categorization of periods, schools, and styles. As much as I loved learning about art through various historical and analytic lenses, I was intrigued by the children's apparently more direct, primary experience of art and its potential for self-understanding. As I read more artists' comments about their own

Head of a Woman, 1962, Pablo Picasso, executed by Paul Nesjar in 1971

art, it seemed that regression to a childlike state was essential to the creation of much art and also the appreciation of it. I saw that adults can, through interacting with art in a direct way, experience raw feelings, relearn primary process thinking, and achieve mental clarity—all of which can be used for self-improvement and to enhance relationships.

Only later as a psychiatrist, however, did I become convinced that art's healing potential could be stronger than any pill. Subsequently, I devised then implemented the various functions of art healing. I defined art healing as a tool for self-realization, symptom reduction, personality improvement, and emotional healing, as well as a grounded and supportive stance toward life in general. Since visual art so directly and expeditiously liberates thoughts, feelings, and memories, I discovered it can yield more incisive insights about patients' inner environments than any verbal interpretation I could give them. I envisioned that people wanting deepened understanding of their own psyches and increased emotional stability beyond the exhausting yet critical work of psychotherapy, might seek out art at a museum, gallery, or might search for less rarefied locales, such as a sculpture park or a funky restaurant or café. Such art spaces then would become not only places of welcome diversion from dreary everyday life—nice temperature- and humidity-controlled or otherwise pleasant spaces with a peaceful rhythm, and perhaps the reassuring presence of silent, uniformed guards—but also potentially challenging, even painfully evocative, providing both a mirror of inner senses and a window on personal history.

The ideas advocated in this book evolved as well from observing the art healing of patients. As they talked about artworks with which they had interacted, I noticed that their orientation to creativity had shaped their therapeutic dialogue, including views of their personal issues. Frequently they showed me a work of art so I could better understand their situation, mood, or thought on a level not easily expressed in words. Even more insightful, though, were their heartfelt, intricate descriptions of artworks. When looking at specific works of art, the patients seemed to move quickly to investigate core issues, and thus we could expedite therapeutic work.

After noting the therapeutic value of interacting with artworks, I deliberately asked patients to seek out and interact with artworks using self-guiding questions and report their experiences. For some, I suggested certain works or artists based on what I knew about the patients' personal histories, conflicts, and deficits. Later these individuals felt more confident in their ability to find on their own the types of artworks that could excite important revelations.

During such observations, I learned that healing through art healing occurs as we allow art to blend with our emotions, establishing a communion with something that catalyzes responses but is not necessarily archetypal. Similar to the way good therapy leads to understanding the inner self and provides support, catharsis, and a sense of well-being on bad days or during foul moods, art healing can become a useful healing practice, teaching us to confront and better comprehend thoughts, feelings, and patterns of behavior. Much as an art historian attempts to make sense of a particular work's significance by giving close attention to its historical context and style, through examining our reactions to specific artworks we might visualize more clearly our deficits and conflicts, as well as ways to overcome them. In this way, practicing art healing forces us to fill in the blanks regarding our lives the way an art collector might gradually fill up a house with personally meaningful works of art. And later, when we reflect on the initial experience with an artwork that helped us on a particular day, we can further deepen our understanding of its effect on us and reinforce healing. Or by returning to an artwork that may have inspired us in the past, we may be able to better comprehend its transformative influence at the time and explore how we may have since changed. If we have training in art history, we might use our knowledge to find works that resonate with us, or make us recall memories of problems experienced at times in our lives. Since artworks are as diverse as fingerprints, anyone can find works that reflect specific personal dilemmas and evoke informative responses.

To experience art healing's full potential to provide personal insights and healing requires a willingness to remain open to various kinds of art, both contemporary and traditional, no matter how bizarre or unconventional the medium, and to allow sufficient time for it to unlock our more elusive thoughts and feelings. Although we may identify more easily with contemporary art that reflects life in the modern world, art from centuries ago might, by contrast, make us see problems of modern life and provide a view of our stressed psyche. For instance, the image of a neoclassical idyll might inform us of a place we've never been in our lives, a landscape of both external and internal peace. Further, for art healing the art does not have to be unfamiliar to catalyze self-reflection. Even the most well-known pieces of art might hold mystery for us when we interact with them with the intention of accessing our inner selves. For example, the smile of the Mona Lisa, even from behind a sheet of Plexiglas and a forest of admirers, might function as a self-administered Rorschach inkblot test, eliciting feelings that float to the surface of our awareness as we connect with the work's gestural ambivalence, causing us to recognize our own gnawing uncertainty, suppressed penchant for mischief, or embarrassment at living with an unsightly physical flaw.

Compared with existing modes of understanding art or using it for therapeutic purposes, art healing employs a unique approach. Unlike art criticism or art history, it focuses more on the personal context of the viewer than on the historical context or aesthetic evaluation of artworks. In contrast to art therapy, where healing occurs as patients create artworks that reflect core issues and feelings, art healing involves interactions with the artworks of others to catalyze personal insights and transformation, with the works ultimately becoming the viewers' creations. Finally, art healing substitutes a visual dialogue between patient and therapist for psychotherapy's verbal give and take, thereby facilitating a potentially faster and greater understanding of a patient's inner self.

Illustrating the book's descriptions of art healing are examples of many types of visual art, as well as numerous scenarios that may reflect the situations of diverse readers. The scenarios, composites of actual and hypothetical circumstances, depict real psychological issues. Many of the art seekers' interactions with specific artworks recount personal dilemmas and conditions existing within the psyches of high-functioning people, including my patients, friends, family members, and myself. The various scenarios give testament to the nuclear power of unprocessed emotion, the universal human penchant for irrationality—regardless of background, profession, or household income—and the nearly ubiquitous need for healing to one degree or another. Despite my patients' and others' contributions, *Art Healing* does not represent a controlled, scientific study; its aim is not to prove but to teach.

This book is for anyone who is in search of healing through increased self-reflection and awareness. The professional community of psychiatrists, psychologists, and masters-level therapists might use this approach to help themselves as well as their patients since the practice of art healing has the potential to catalyze personal transformation for a more productive and joyous life.

introduction

ART HEALING CAN BE USED AS A TOOL FOR EMOTIONAL HEALING, PERSONALITY IM-provement, self-realization, and the reduction of symptoms resulting from depressed mood, inappropriate anger, compulsive behavior, existential loneliness, debilitating anxiety, or thwart-ed desire. Through interacting with artworks, it is possible to gain mastery over emotional pain, psycho-logical traumas, and paralyzing mental stagnation to attain a broader, more positive perspective on life.

One of my own recent experiences with art healing provides a straightforward example of how art can help heal an emotional wound. A work of art assisted me in quelling anger, integrating raw emotion, and gaining insights about behavior patterns. As would be true in any high-quality psycho-therapy, the contextual details of the incident, described below, play a critical role in understanding my experience.

After spending most of a Sunday morning apart from my wife and children, I met them at a Borders bookstore. As they were standing in line, I discovered that they had just purchased a replacement for my children's Guitar Hero CD-ROM, which only a short while earlier had been carelessly damaged. Angry, I asked my wife rhetorically how a child can appreciate the value of money when there is no time span between when something is broken and replaced to underscore the feelings arising from the absence of a prized possession. I could tell by the tone of my wife's response that she understood the logic of my argument, but she explained how the money used to replace the children's game disc had come out of the holiday gift money their grandfather had given them and that the children had agreed to spend the money replacing the disc. Despite her reasonable explanation, my anger persisted, prompting me to escape to Boston for the rest of the day to be by myself.

By the time I made it to Boston's Institute of Contemporary Art and found Cornelia Parker's *Hanging Fire (Suspected Arson)*, 1999,[2] I was not as exasperated as earlier but still felt tension in my head and chest and a queasy sensation in my stomach. I looked at the huge cube of charred wood suspended by individual strands hanging from a rectangular wire mesh on the ceiling. The pattern created by the pieces of wood in space—with the larger charred pieces congregating around the center and lower portion and progressively smaller pieces suspended closer to the upper part and the edges of the cube—made it appear as though a blast had been captured instantaneously. Although I had seen *Hanging Fire* before and thought it clever and interesting, as I encountered it in my agitated frame of mind it had more immediacy and power for me. My weakened mental state, no longer supported by my usual defense mechanisms, had made me vulnerable so that I could more easily interact with it. And the space created by the suspended strands of burnt wood offered permeability, providing an opening for me to enter. As I merged with the work and, for a moment, became the fire, I felt myself transforming through a kind of sensual catalysis. The fire—set surreptitiously on purpose to achieve a destructive end, according to the work's parenthetical title—reflected my short fuse and inclination toward self-righteousness.

In this context, I realized that my feelings were disproportionately strong compared with the relatively minor precipitating event of my family's purchase and that my explosive anger came not just from the inciting event but also from earlier traumas. Focusing more closely on *Hanging Fire*, I could graphically see in four dimensions the potential of self-destructive feelings such as anger. I wondered if I was an "arsonist," intermittently and recklessly setting fires within myself and near others, unable to reverse the damage once the emotions were unleashed. I had always been scared of the capacity of violent mindless anger to ruin one's life—professional career, intimate relationships, connection to one's children—in a single careless moment.

Hanging Fire (Suspected Arson), 1999, Cornelia Parker
Courtesy of the artist and Frith Street Gallery, London
Photo: Steve White

Most importantly, I had the insight that within my rage there existed a hidden image, like a faded photographic negative of my childhood, which I surmised played a central role in my reaction. Reflecting further, I remembered a time when my grandparents had bought me a toy I had coveted for at least forty weeks before my mother had smashed it. Merlin, the bright red phone-shaped electronic game, did not just die when she flung it against a wall in a fit of rage; it became damaged, afterward acting weird, with random lights flashing and dying cow sounds emanating from its speaker. Crushed, I had absorbed the anger into my being like a sponge. Yet to survive within the logic of my family of origin, I had been required to hide the incident from my grandparents and consequently suppress my emotions about it. This realization about my past experience was sufficient to dissipate my rage. Evidently, *Hanging Fire* had served as a container for my anger, so I could transmute its energy into positive insights. It is no wonder that the memory of interacting with *Hanging Fire* and subsequent release of rage, as my earlier trauma was healed by the work's power, has remained with me.

Although I was able to gain sudden insights into my past by linking a fit of anger to a work of art, the healing experienced was not achieved by mere mood-matching but seems to have been a higher-order revelation, offering a slideshow of past experience, as if an intensely bright lightbulb had been placed in a long-defunct "projection machine" within me.[3] It was through this merge with *Hanging Fire* that I proved to myself the immediacy with which art can be used to reduce pain and transform inner states.

As I learned that day in Boston, and many others have learned in a wide variety of settings, by choosing to interact with the most personally compelling artworks you can find, then exploring how their various aspects resonate with your thoughts, feelings, and behavioral patterns through self-reflection, you can reveal unconscious desires and painful conflicts as though standing naked in front of a mirror. Then you may be able to resolve issues for a healthier life instead of dealing with ongoing emotional distress by engaging in destructive behaviors, such as compulsive eating, irresponsible spending, revolving-door relationships, or comparing and contrasting yourself with your status- and fashion-addled peers. Such behaviors can trap you in an energy-sapping eddy, spinning you like a potter's wheel in perpetual motion.

Finding and identifying the right kind of art that speaks to your inner self is an important part of art healing. Recognition of such artworks occurs when they stir a feeling deep inside you that declares to the art—whether a painting, sculpture, video, film, performance, multimedia installation, outdoor earthwork, or conceptual piece—"It's you that I need!" Alternatively, recognition of a potentially useful artwork can also happen if it repels you, signifying that it has "pushed a button." Consequently, as a new art seeker, look for what particularly appeals to you or, conversely, what disgusts you. In either case, artwork that elicits strong emotion indicates it has penetrated the callused skin of your unconscious. Your reaction might reactivate a memory of something painful you have long known on a subconscious level but which your mind has kept walled off to protect you from negativity and thwarted desire. Equally important is the ability to be vulnerable when interacting with the artwork. The more you give of yourself to an artwork, the more you receive from it. For maximum benefit, you will want to interact with the right piece at the right time, depending on your situation and emotional state, and remain open to its potential effect on you.

Art healing is at once deeply personal and dependent upon others—a practice in which you rely on someone else's expression to help you better come to terms with tears in your own psychic fabric. Artworks can provide validation for personal healing in a way that parallels work with a psychotherapist. In psychotherapy, whether individual or group, a patient internalizes validations from one or more people to gain insights into personal conflicts and behaviors and increase consciousness and healing. Similarly, artworks, though inanimate objects, have the power to provide something the art seeker is unable to provide, to validate conflicts, stimulate self-expression, and thus catalyze healing. Further, the process of discovery in art healing is akin to the use of homeopathic cures or addiction medicine,[4] because, like them, it employs the notion that like treats like. Certain aspects of art on which you focus both reflect and remedy your problems—whether they relate to insatiable desires, bad habits, myopic compulsions, inconsolable anxieties, relational disturbance, or transgenerational wounds. Harsh self-admonitions rarely accomplish much, while engaging in enjoyable pursuits can help you. Connecting with art that mirrors your problems but also provides pleasure can supply momentary relief and also lead to increased consciousness of issues that need healing through recognition of links between thoughts and feelings evoked by an artwork and the complex canvas or intricate sculptural design of your own inner world.

Healing that occurs as a result of art healing can take many forms, from simple comfort to discomforting reassessment of past traumas. Like the warm touch of the arm of a stranger sitting next to you on an airplane during a white-knuckling turbulent descent, art can provide surprising comfort when there seems to be little available from other sources. Finally, although art healing does not promise connection with the spiritual dimension, the great mysteries have so inspired art through the ages that you may have an opportunity to tap into this dimension by focusing on artworks that are most meaningful for you and have such potential.

Moreover, art healing can give you a sense of vulnerable and frequently wounded human beings who often face isolation. Such a connection to others by experiencing art can provide a feeling of being part of humanity. For example, paintings on the cave walls at Lascaux, as well as all art produced since then, says to the art seeker: "Someone was here and made this, someone with human needs and vision!" Consequently, through art healing you are not, contrary to appearances, having a conversation with only yourself but also talking with others as you link your mind with the artists or viewers who have felt pain, glee, boredom, ecstasy, loneliness, or inspiration while creating or looking at the same artworks.

Although the benefits of art healing can be similar to those of more conventional forms of psychotherapy, it is important to distinguish art healing from them. For starters, art healing can be differentiated from the style of psychotherapy known as art therapy by virtue of the fact that in art therapy patients create their own art to gain insights into their conflicts and feelings while in art healing people employ artworks already created by others. Given the variety of artworks available for such use, the only thing individuals need to do is respond to them in the vibrant medium of thoughts and feelings. This conserves energy and provides space for personal creativity without the need to don a smock, soften clay, or mix paint. Instead of taking the time to drip watercolor onto paper to reconnect with childhood wounds, as you might be asked to do by an art therapist, in art healing you can enjoy real-time exploration in galleries, museums, or at home in front of a television screen or computer monitor, then reflect on its meaning for your own inner life, while perhaps jotting down some thoughts for future reference.

For people living in the wired world of the twenty-first century who are short on time and require fast results, personal use of others' artworks can be a highly practical means of healing. Such an approach—involving adaptation to existing structures, or, from a geek's view, open source subroutines you can paste into your own code—may be a more realistic option for change. Contemporary art itself reflects this model, with the postmodernist idea of appropriation and the notion that originality is either a myth (since it has all been done before) or a unique combination of pieces of history. In music, this is what might be called sampling, a riff here or there originally appearing years ago in other songs and later incorporated into newly created compositions.

In addition, art healing may provide a welcome alternative for people who view typical art therapy as juvenilizing in its approach. To them, using crayons to "draw how you feel" might seem forced, simplistic, and incapable of capturing past experience that begs for examination and healing. For instance, instead of becoming frustrated while attempting to express a lack of connection to others with what ultimately appears as cartoony stick figures floating above a desert wasteland, an individual might study the works of an artist like Edward Hopper, famous for capturing the angst of nocturnal city dwellers surrounding a lunch counter in *Nighthawks,* to more precisely examine her mental pain.

Art healing also does not require focus on traditional psychoanalytic symbolism. In contrast to psychiatrist Carl Jung's emphasis on artworks that reflect archetypal images from the collective unconscious, art healing's power does not stem from universal interpretations. Although Jung's idea that the secret of great art lies in its ability to "transmute personal destiny into the destiny of mankind" allowing "humanity to find a refuge from every peril and to outlive the longest night"[5] provides a useful perspective on art, its presence is not necessary for effective art healing. Over the last century, classic analytical practitioners often interpreted artwork in terms of universal symbolism and correlated certain shapes with particular meanings, but such rigid interpretations often led to oversimplification or even absurdity. For example, depictions of elongated objects or negative spaces invariably became associated with the person's underlying sexual conflicts. When a twelve-year-old emotionally disturbed boy drew an open-mouthed gray whale named Moby Dick in an art therapy session, the therapist found it an "obvious" expression of hidden, even sinister, sexual meanings of which the artist was unconscious:

> The whole whale can be interpreted as one giant penis, conceived as a dangerous weapon with teeth. The whale's mouth, on the other hand, can also be interpreted as a vagina dentata, devouring the male organ.[6]

Even the name of the whale is recruited for confirmation of underlying sexual conflict, leading to the conclusion that the boy's masturbatory fantasies are "dangerous and evil" and that he sees his mother as a whore, which may or may not accurately depict the boy's feelings. By contrast, the relative absence of universal symbols in an artwork does not inhibit or lessen its potential to catalyze personal reflection and healing. Your connection to even the smallest apparently nonsymbolic image might bring you closer to insights about your parents, perhaps causing you to see them as blamelessly beholden to the cultural mores of the times.

Nor does art healing require understanding or resonating with the artist's intention in creating artworks. Instead, art healing involves the personal appropriation of artworks regardless of their creators' intended meaning or audience. In fact, in art healing, an object in a work of art, such as a snow shovel, becomes twice removed from its original identity and function: the item initially becomes a "found object" and is then further removed when the art seeker treats the work of art itself as an object for personal use. Life's million-fold nuances of experience and emotion—from the silliness of a consumer society where single apples are packaged in clear plastic bags to the solemnity of personal pain from deep psychological trauma—are all reflected in art, ready for you to connect with and use for personal healing, conscious engagement of personal signification, or meaning-making. If a person happens to find that an artwork depicting salamis has a sexual meaning, then such an interpretation has significance for that individual, although for someone else the same image might trigger positive memories of sharing sandwiches with her grandfather at Katz's Deli.

Art healing also differs from more traditional modes of psychotherapy occurring with a therapist. Except for the few obligatory pieces of art displayed as decoration in a therapist's office, or the passé projective test of Rorschach inkblots, talk therapy limits itself to images created in the minds of the participants. By contrast, art healing focuses on visual qualities to directly evoke personal responses. This method of healing thus relies upon the untapped resource of vision as a critical therapeutic tool. Since we generally use the eyes to interpret external phenomena and employ the words *looking* and *seeing* when speaking about inner experiences, it makes sense that art healing has us concentrate on vision for interpreting our inner world.

Art healing also has a different goal from art history and art criticism, although it can be practiced while interacting with these disciplines, especially while reading illustrated materials associated with them. For example, while people with little or no background in art may have trouble comprehending the challenging articles in a publication like *Artforum International,* the most re-

spected international journal of contemporary art criticism and exhibition reviews, individuals pursu-
ing art healing may find the luscious, large-format images and statements by artists invaluable for
their purposes. For instance, in a recent *Artforum* essay by artist Nick Mauss on the art of Jochen
Klein, Mauss recognizes how art provides personal therapeutic value and describes the interaction
common to art healing:

> The paintings are moments of quiet, pauses drawn out to a complete stillness in which I find
> myself. I am reminded by these works of the potential for paintings to embarrass: I am never sure
> how to behave around them; they seem to know my foibles. Some flirt, or correspond to a recent
> mood, like the ballerina wearing a concerned look as, above, a squall of viscous varnish threatens
> to overcome her. Or like the young man in a pale blue summer shirt, in another painting, who
> looks out at me with great benevolence, emanating such sweet-toothed empathy that every-
> thing around him falls out of focus: distortions of vision induced by great happiness, silliness,
> sadness, love.[7]

Since art healing involves healing through learning, in which an artist's unique expression offers
a novel stimulus, its success hinges on emotional availability and breadth of receptivity—the smaller
your solar panel, the less electricity you generate. You must be open to the potential benefits of the
method, to the work of art itself, and to the possibility of making connections between aspects of the
art and yourself. Therefore, when selecting artworks with which to interact, it is important to remain
receptive to subject matter and style rather than insisting that every artwork reflects your personal
taste. You would do well to heed the lament of the gallery owner who noted that when prospective art
owners shy away from pieces that do not at first seem to match their temperaments or personal styles
they miss works that might challenge them and initiate new experiences.

Art healing becomes a richer experience if you do not neglect works that elicit negative emotions or appear to conflict with your beliefs. Recent research by psychologists Paul Silvia and Elizabeth Brown, who studied negative emotions such as anger and disgust occurring in response to art, explored how these emotions reflected the viewers' values: "Negative aesthetic emotions are in the eye of the appraiser—they come from evaluations of how art relates to one's goals and values—so even cheery, benign art can make people mad."[8] The authors concluded that anger tends to be elicited when viewers interpret a work as incongruent with their values and when they suspect the artist has done this on purpose to evoke a response. In contrast, disgust emerges as an emotional response when the work is incongruent with the viewer's values and provides unpleasant imagery. Keeping this in mind, to exercise what may be surely atrophic muscles of visual and emotional receptivity and reassess values you may even want to investigate works in which you have had no past interest or have found unpleasant, ugly, or likely to arouse anger or disgust, even if you ultimately choose to focus on more familiar types of art. You needn't worry about having to spend hours with something you find incomprehensible, boring, or uninspiring, because you are in control.

Moreover, artworks, through choice of medium and artistic expression, can make even normally ugly subjects beautiful. Umberto Eco, editor of *History of Beauty*, writes: "Although ugly creatures and things exist, art has the power to portray them in a beautiful way, and the Beauty of this imitation makes Ugliness acceptable. . . . The Ugliness that repels us in nature exists, but it becomes acceptable and even pleasurable in the art that expresses and shows 'beautifully' the ugliness of Ugliness."[9] Thus art in art healing becomes more "beautiful" the greater its personal gift for the art seeker, much as Shel Silverstein's classic Giving Tree grows in beauty the more it gives of itself to a human beneficiary. Once you've had a chance to feel something, even something unpleasant, try to figure out why; ask yourself appropriate questions to discover threads that can lead you into the labyrinth of your emotions and psyche so you can begin the work of uncovering conflicts and healing old wounds. Above all, avoid prejudging the emotions you think specific artworks are intended to elicit. Allowing yourself to be in the presence of the art without judgment will permit you to maintain the openness needed to take advantage of art healing's full potential. You might find, for example, that you have always gone out of your way to avoid surrealist art, perhaps turned off by distorted images of glistening hypertro- phied limbs or eyebrows comprised entirely of swarming termites. Or maybe you are less squeamish about the bizarre appearance of familiar objects than you are disgusted by what seems to you the artist's attempt to produce an eerie effect. But regardless of the reason for your repulsion, it may be advantageous to reconsider such artworks as an exercise in facing what you find unpleasant to experi- ence psychological benefits. Despite your first impressions of artworks, your feelings engendered by them might nevertheless be helpful in personal healing.

As an example of self-discovery through an artwork that evokes revulsion, an art seeker might probe a painting by the "hyperrealist" painter Valerio Carrubba, who melds portraiture with anatomi- cally precise internal organs of the same subject to potentially nauseating effect. But pushing past an initial gut-wrenching reaction might afford an opportunity to discover not only insights about the self but unanticipated beauty in the work, such as admiration for both the skilled rendering of muscle, blood vessels, connective tissue, nerves, and organs and how they stand in sharp, unsettling contrast to their surroundings. More specifically, one Carrubba painting, *Bird Rib,* 2007,[10] features a man-cum-anatomy lesson, presumably skiing on a slope, with the background of snow-covered mountains, ski lift, and shower of red corpuscles falling neatly from the hand of a person-as-sun. The bizarre juxtaposition of surgical rendering with fantastical outdoor landscape might prompt consideration of the contrast between surfaces and inner depths, especially the inner machinery of the body and unconscious mind, often camouflaged by the skin and conscious awareness. Thoughtful examination of this work might also call attention to what might "really be going on" in the inner life of an art seeker, much as when a precocious child takes apart a refrigerator to reveal how that metal and plastic box chills his food.

Successful art healing requires not only a willingness to face what you most want to avoid in your inner life but also a readiness to observe details as closely as a child would. Give yourself the time and space to play with art as though you were a child, so you can interact with it in an uninhibited manner. Adults can use art to play—as children use toys to practice for the demands of adult life—to facilitate connections between aspects of inner and outer worlds. You can expand your perspective on both the art and your inner environment by doing such things as pretending that you were the artist of a given artwork or that you are the artwork itself, employing or embodying its colors, shapes, textures, and style in role-playing. Or you can imagine you are Indiana Jones on a serial adventure excavating art's Temple of Doom, containing, at various levels, conflicting motivations and emotional detritus to reveal ways you can broaden your perception and heal. Then use art healing to confront inner obstacles or conflicts that may have originated in your childhood or youth as you were molded by parental or societal influences.

Having mastered such attitudes, you can increase your options for healing by recognizing patterns in artworks and their relevance to your own patterns of thoughts, emotions, or conflicts. For example, as an art seeker you might notice in a portrait of a young woman a curly lock of hair that resonates with what seems to be a swirl of water draining from a huge bathtub, a motif not only having visual interest but complementing the text that appears as a thought bubble over the subject's head: "I don't care! I'd rather sink—than call Brad for help!"[11] Then you might recognize how the motif represents a pattern in your own life, such as how the swirling in the art reflects a dizzying spiral of friends taken in by your charm but who ultimately disappear from your life. In such moments of recognition, works of art are valued more for their personal meanings and less for style or execution.

Art effects positive psychological change in different ways depending on the type of artwork. For example, John Szarkowski, in his landmark photography exhibit at the Museum of Modern Art, entitled "Mirrors and Windows: American Photography Since 1960," distinguishes between photographs that function as mirrors and those that function as windows—providing a view of the subjective inner self or the objective outer world. Works either presented elements of the outside world containing "discoverable patterns of intrinsic meaning"[12] or were "dependent upon our own understandings"[13] and thus mirrored inner values and environment. This distinction is illustrated photographically in the difference between the works of Minor White, whose images mirror the photographer's internal world, and those of Robert Frank, whose images form windows onto the external world. In art healing, a self-concerned and self-reflective practice, artworks perhaps integrate both functions, serving as a two-way mirror: one reflecting the outer world and the other the inner self. Such categorization is limiting, however, because many artworks potentially serve multiple functions. For instance, through art healing you may not only hold a mirror to your current self or open a window to the world as you conceive it; you may also get a view of a parallel world containing your alter ego—or doppelgänger— offering a symbolic expression of your present angst-ridden form. For example, in identifying with the darkness-enshrouded lobster poacher in Andrew Wyeth's *Night Hauling*,[14] whose lamp backlights the stolen wooden trap and the stream of water gushing from its bottom, you might recognize your emotional double and through reflection discover new truths about yourself. You may, for instance, sense that your perception of yourself as a crafty criminal concerned about eluding apprehension is a grossly inaccurate self-characterization and determine to repudiate this recurring, corrosive sense of yourself more fully in the future.

Whether serving as a window, mirror, or a combination of the two, artworks can catalyze profound experiences due to the interactive effect of art healing. Art healing has the power to broaden the experience of viewing art by imbuing the artworks with meaning they may not have alone, adding to the aesthetic experience while at the same time encouraging exploration into the more metaphorical aspects of the self through initiating mental dialogue with yourself as well as with the art.

To derive the most from art healing, it is important to understand its six functions: aesthetic, symbolic, participatory, permeability, transformative, and memory. The first function of art healing, the aesthetic function, relates to interacting with an artwork's physical qualities, rather than its subject matter like form, line, color, and texture. Such aesthetic qualities have often been described by philosophers and art historians as what elevates a work from a mere craft to art. Form, line, color, and texture may combine with subject matter to yield an inspired creation that "calls you," stimulating your senses, awakening deep feelings at your core that compel you to reel in its presence, and sometimes even to experience the divine.

To pursue the aesthetic function, let your eye wander of its own volition over artworks, experiencing how line intersects with line or some materials seem to take on qualities of other materials without categorizing or criticizing what is before you so you can be open to spontaneous experiences. For example, lush, soft-appearing carpet might magically reveal its true composition as a bed of tiny upturned pins. When something soothes you, or jibes with your color preferences, feel it fully. If there is a sense of beauty emanating from found objects of Mylar balloons with cartoon figures streaming horizontally across a blue video sky,[15] or an installation resembling a faux science experiment where live plants are grown in tanks of golf balls and fed with Gatorade,[16] take it all in without making judgments, such as denigrating the seeming banality of the ideas contained within the art. As you look at a work from this purely sensual point of view, see if its external characteristics correspond to any of your thoughts or feelings capable of enlightening you about aspects of yourself.

The second function of art healing, the symbolic function, has to do with the ways ideas, images, and symbols serve as hooks on which to hang your emotional baggage. Meaning emerges at various moments during an art healing session as you make mental associations between particular symbols in the art and your feelings, behaviors, or patterns. Gleaning meaning from images in art—perhaps a torn shoe, a mountain, or a disfigured nose—differs from absorbing feelings emanating from an artwork's forms, colors, or textures.

Two by Two, 2007, Yeshe Parks

The symbolic function complements the aesthetic function since it is about how ideas, images, or symbols in art, as opposed to the physical qualities of artworks, trigger self-reflection and healing. Studying art's symbols and other recognizable elements can initiate self-reflection, helping you reaffirm what you sense is true about yourself and transform aspects of your personality to live more in sync with your hopes for the future.

Although this function can be effective while interacting with abstract art since certain forms, streaks, or dots might remind you of specific objects and thus initiate self-reflection, the symbolic function seems to work best with art that is at least somewhat representational. As an example, consider *Two by Two*, 2007, by Yeshe Parks.[17] This complex, bizarre scene of creatures requires a long, uninterrupted time to search out the ideas, images, and symbols within it. A number of animal figures and one man emerge from mouths like a psychedelic riff on a biologist's diagram explaining how a food chain works. All the creatures originate from one hollow horn of a humanoid's strange spacesuit. The suit's freakishly long arms rest on the ground in a way reminiscent of a pair of didgeridoos. Abstracted elephant trunks, a group of haggard people, and a solitary figure perched on a precipice float within a slate blue sea or sky. Drawings of the humans suggest leopard spots, zebra stripes, and tiger patterns. Curved fingerlike "guts" visible in the spacesuit's midsection, collaged text "islands" or "clouds" formed from torn dictionary pages, an elephant trunk plugging a man's mouth, and a figure scaling a crooked ladder add to the work's inscrutability. Its very obscurity, however, allows viewers to project their own meanings from a multitude of possibilities. For instance, you might gain insight about an inhibiting metaphoric food chain causing you to consistently fall prey to predator coworkers. Alternatively, you might discover that your parents' knee-jerk fundamentalist response to your life's every frayed edge or gray area is no longer either useful or relevant to how you choose to live.

The symbolic function is the one that most closely resembles a psychological test, such as a Rorschach inkblot or Thematic Apperception Test that encourages self-revealing projection. Using art as a guide to free associate and recognize problems in your life by focusing on some scene, figure, image, design, or action is akin to using a Rorschach or other projective psychological test. Freud believed in the healing benefits of free association, and to make the most of art healing it is necessary to develop this skill just as you would exercise to develop muscles. When a psychologist employs a projective test like a Rorschach or Thematic Apperception Test, the patient is asked to "read into" an inkblot or a sketch of a scene to reveal inner feelings, behaviors, and patterns, or possible conflicts. Similarly, in art healing an image or design might remind you of thoughts or feelings that guide you gradually to focus on deeper psychological issues. While identification of an inkblot abstraction, by itself, may not provide much in the way of "interpretive richness,"[18] if these descriptions are accompanied by a context, such as a black bat that's swooping down to feed off young children, this may add sufficient information to determine that the person feels vulnerable and may see in the inkblot his history of victimization. Alternatively, the reading of another inkblot by an individual who perpetrates damage might be: "It looks like a squashed bug, like I just put my foot on it."[19]

In comparing art healing with such psychological tools, you will learn to appreciate that your reactions to particular images or symbols in art have the potential to yield core psychological information about you, especially when the context connected with them is taken into consideration. For instance, in isolation an image of a peach pit may not seem to hold much value, but if you allow it to conjure up memories of a day when you discovered one beneath the sand at Jones Beach after a traumatic breakup with your partner, it serves a symbolic function. Using this example to further differentiate between the aesthetic and symbolic functions, it becomes apparent that while the aesthetic function would inspire associations with the pock-marked appearance of the peach pit, viewing it instead as a symbolic object might awaken a memory of a math teacher with acne-ravaged skin who once made out with your mother on the night of a parent-teacher conference. The symbolic function's emphasis on emotional content rather than physical qualities helps art seekers better understand the roots of anxieties and problematic personality features in order to heal them.

The third function of art healing, the participatory function, is concerned with how art pulls you into its world, either indirectly through the attraction of some particular element or directly through engagement in the artwork itself, such as a work depicting a leap onto gymnastics mats.[20] In considering how you are called to participate and noting your responses, you can gain insights about yourself. And while the aesthetic function occurs when the art seeker is a passive receiver of physical stimuli such as textures and colors that may elicit feelings, the participatory function is initiated as the viewer actively merges with the art's story, becoming an extension of the art.

In the participatory function, what the art looks like takes a backseat to how you participate in it and what the participation evokes in you. For example, when an artwork encourages you to enter a special space and look at rows of yellow foam "mattresses" on which impressions of reclining human figures have been created by what was "ripped," you may examine the art like a doctor entering a ward in an antique hospital[21]—a perspective that might cause you to consider the meaning of your obsessive thoughts about illness and death. Or when interacting with an artwork that calls on you to come behind a wall and choose a white clublike object to swing around in front of a mirror,[22] you might reflect on your aggressive tendencies or lack of assertiveness. Even when an art seeker's participation entails something less concrete, like deciphering a narrative thread from one hundred small pencil drawings arranged rectilinearly on a wall, the mental activity involved reflects the participatory function. In effect, the participatory function offers the art seeker evocative experiences that do not necessarily require jumping into a foam pit, such as the potential for inclusion in the experience of others, exercising the mind as an impetus for trying new things, and an invitation to become the art itself.

The fourth function of art healing, the permeability function, relates to an artwork's ability to penetrate your psychological defense mechanisms, making it easier to confront painful feelings and memories to aid healing. Compared with the participatory function, it works on a deeper, psychological level, even on your subconscious mind. Typically this requires a shock to penetrate the walls you put up to protect your vulnerable self. As an analogy, you cannot perform abdominal surgery without cutting through the skin, fascia, and muscle to get to the guts.

When art healing serves the permeability function, boundaries between you and the art dissolve either gradually or abruptly. To facilitate permeability, look for an opening where you can insert yourself into the art. The mechanism of permeability, the interlacing of art and individual, is like two embryonic stem cells that initially grow as neighbors sharing a membrane, but which, due to a common purpose of proliferating tissue of a specific organ, eventually merge.

In effect, the permeability function involves specific aspects of your past, present, and anticipated future rather than the participatory function's effect on your whole being, and when art healing serves the permeability function the artwork has the capacity to cause more immediate reflection on core issues as opposed to more superficial ones. For example, when viewing a photographic image of a young married couple swinging from ropes within the confines of an apparently sparse bedroom space with no bed,[23] you may see an elegant pairing, interpreting it as something you never experienced as a child of a single parent or in an intimate relationship with a lover. At such times, you will likely experience moments of interconnections with and dissociation from an artwork, much as you might after getting off an airplane in a place you have never seen before and feeling as if you are in a dream. It becomes like improvisational theater that you produce for an audience of one, yourself.

The fifth function of art healing, the transformative function, is concerned with reconfiguration, or renewal. Of all the art healing functions, this one is the most alchemical, inviting a deep merging with an artwork that encourages you to broaden your perspective and alter your internal dynamics in such a way that you will never again be exactly the same person as before interacting with it. Using such art as catalyst might result in a breaking free from destructive behavior patterns or a major overhaul of parts of your personality.

If you have been working on core issues in psychotherapy or using other art healing functions, this function may help you intensify a process already in motion. Whatever symptoms of anxiety or issues of identity or coping you have before interaction with the art will become less powerful after the transformation. For example, a deepening connection to a particular work of art may help manifest results from a psychic process, such as after nine months of therapy, finally extracting yourself emotionally from a passive-aggressive, manipulative ex-husband.

Finally, the sixth function of art healing, the memory function, has to do with two things: how art healing triggers memories as a prelude to transformation and how specific interactions with art can be deposited in your memory bank to save for reinforcing further insights to promote healing. The memory function permits you to keep interacting with certain artworks long after the closing announcement on the museum's PA system, allowing you to summon art healing experiences when you need them most—in times of crisis or when grappling with negative thoughts and emotions. Further, this function involves not just recalling encounters with artworks but psychically retaining the essence of such experiences to sustain transformations and facilitate ongoing healing. You might visualize this as the essence of your positive transformation encapsulated in the form of a crystal that you can slip into your mind's pocket to carry into the future as a reminder of certain feelings and ideas, or as a source of new power. Alternatively, you might see this nugget as the essence of your core conflicts, the negative aspects you have confronted and discarded to make way for greater creativity and peace.

|||||||||

To make art healing work for you, access art on a regular basis so that over time you develop a rapport with it and engage in more interactions possibly resulting in transformation. Fortunately, sources of art for art healing are everywhere, not only in museums and galleries but also in books, art magazines, films, and on the Internet. You might begin by visiting a local museum or gallery, or looking for sculpture you have previously ignored in a public space or in a building where you work. Although it's a good bet that New York, Paris, and London afford ample opportunity to find the latest, cutting-edge contemporary art, good art that calls to you might come from relatively unknown artists in your town or small city, off the radar of the art cognoscenti. Though many of the examples in this book come from well-established galleries and museums in art-oriented cities, some examples of lesser-known artists and galleries are also included. And while a printed image of a work of art often differs from the experience of seeing it up close in a gallery, for people living far from urban centers this is an acceptable way to engage in art healing, as is art based exclusively on the medium of the Internet. Finally, if you do not have an art cinema available to you, or a museum with black-box video or film projections, you might use art films available through Netflix. Although viewing many different types of movies might be therapeutic, the focus for art healing should be on nonnarrative avant-garde or experimental films because they tend to better catalyze an art seeker's creativity and self-reflection than the standard plot-driven Hollywood fare.

No matter what sources of art you use for art healing, it helps if your surroundings are quiet. It is difficult to interact with art in a profound way at a crowded museum or art fair. This became obvious to me while attending the famous Armory Art Fair in New York at Pier 94, where I felt I might as well have been twenty blocks south at the New York Auto Show. By contrast, when I went to the back hallway of the American Academy of Arts and Letters on 155th Street, I had time and space to quietly contemplate fantastic art, gradually becoming conscious of sensations and thoughts as they streamed out of my mind and then onto the paper in my notebook. Indeed, you might consider keeping a notebook handy to augment your art healing experience. The healing process you may undertake while interacting in such peaceful places resembles that achieved through participation in different kinds of psychotherapy.

Art healing can work well with art of different styles and eras. To know which kind of art to seek for a given problem—such as skewed perspective; painful, unremitting ideas, like viruses, feeding on the mind; obsessive-compulsive symptoms; or problems involving the decision-making process or commitments to a prospective spouse or career path—consider the advantages and disadvantages of using contemporary art, defined by most museums as art produced after World War II, versus works dating back centuries ago, such as Renaissance, medieval, or ancient art. Contemporary art, with its focus on current issues and aesthetics, and its great diversity of concepts and forms reflective of Western culture's pluralism, offers good opportunities for reflection on inner issues but does not do so exclusively. Aside from contemporary art's treatment of specific technologies or concepts unique to our time, such as the Internet, nuclear weapons, or SpongeBob, ideas expressed in contemporary art may also emanate from older art, such as religious art, folk art, or ethnic art of various eras. Interacting with work that already has associations with your past, such as reproductions of religious art that used to hang in your family living room, might unleash a flood of emotions that facilitate healing. For example, Andrea Mantegna's majestic *Calvary* (1457–1460), with its clearly defined rib cages of Jesus and two other crucified victims, caused one man to actually feel the tears he had shed and horror he had felt years ago when authoritarian parents had paddled him raw before a poster of this image. Insights into our modern afflictions, neuroses, and situations tend to emerge more easily from contemporary art, however, which is informed by our world today, than from art more than a few decades old.

Despite the fact that art of all styles and eras can be used successfully for art healing, the following characteristics of contemporary art make it particularly well-suited to the practice: primacy of idea over aesthetics; tendency to encourage viewer participation; eschewal of "technical virtuosity";[24] reflection of the mass media; and self-conscious attention to human and cultural diversity. First, the primacy of idea over aesthetics in much contemporary art—the fact that it is often concerned less with how something looks than with what something means or symbolizes—makes its use as an instrument of art healing of great potential for therapy. The reason for this is that emotions can obscure insights necessary for the best psychotherapeutic results. The Whitney Biennial 2008's *The Areola*[25] is a good example of the primacy of idea in contemporary art. This work, with its moist green peas wiped on the walls, seems disgusting; yet somehow that's the point, and the reactions it elicits may reveal important insights into personal problems.

Contemporary art can also appropriate a work such as Edvard Munch's *The Scream*, a masterpiece of the late nineteenth century, and, by printing it on inflatable, thick plastic balloons, turn it into a new artwork that embodies a specific idea about the way such classic artworks are mass produced and used everywhere in the modern cultural landscape. In much the same way, the self-declared rarefied art of Jeff Koons depends for its value on ideas—even inside jokes—embedded within its banal exteriors. It is the idea behind work such as *Lifeboat*, 1985, an inflatable raft cast entirely from bronze, that makes it appealing enough to move you somewhere beyond a cursory dismissal of his art as clever ploy with no obvious psychic value. The artist himself serves mostly as an "idea man" for a team of people who make, at his direction, such works as an inflatable bunny, a multistory puppy composed of flowers,[26] and a shiny metal balloon dog.[27] When interviewed for the Sundance Channel program *Iconoclasts*, Jeff Koons discussed the value of the idea in his quintessentially contemporary art but, even more pertinent to art healing, acknowledged that art exists—first and foremost—"in the viewer."[28]

In attempting to interact with the ideas contained in contemporary art, it is important not to let the issue of accessibility discourage you from art healing. Even if you have never entered a museum or gallery because you've been afraid you won't understand the highbrow ideas of contemporary art, keep in mind that the driving force behind art healing is having the experience itself. Consequently, approaching artworks that seem intimidating or make you fearful can become your individual brand of art healing. Such testing of your comfort level challenges you to engage with something you might otherwise avoid, and this experience alone might trigger feelings that have been buried and kept your life stagnant. For example, confronting a shape that suggests an erotically charged flesh-colored cleft might not only be a testimony to your openness and commitment to participate in art healing but cause long-suppressed feelings of anger and resentment toward women to surface, providing potential for change. No matter what you end up doing with the art, just your presence expresses a decision to interact with it for your own benefit.

The second characteristic of contemporary art that makes it especially suitable for art healing is its tendency to encourage viewer participation, facilitating a deep connection with personal thoughts and feelings. To have a participatory function, an artwork need not be contemporary or more than two dimensions since a lot of photographs and paintings, as well as noncontemporary artworks, invite viewers to participate. For example, Diego Velazquez's *Las Meninas*, 1656,[29] included a reflection in a background mirror of Spain's royal couple, guaranteeing their participation. A predominant theme in recent art, however, is more literal participation by viewers, whose presence is seen as part of the work. Such works can more easily activate self-reflection and instigate insights that enhance the odds of a beneficial outcome. An example of this kind of work is Walter de Maria's earthwork *The Lightning Field*,[30] where overnight observation from the vantage point of a 1940s homesteader cabin in the New Mexico desert completes the work. This artwork, a series of four hundred stainless steel poles, requires viewer participation to complete it, much as the act of dreaming, as described by psychiatrist Carl Jung, complements the unfinished business of waking life.

Another example of how participation in an artwork might stimulate a connection with salient themes in an art seeker's life is when, upon seeing a wildly chaotic work and recognizing the "mess" of emotions inside himself due to painful childhood experiences hibernating inside the dark corner of his psyche, such as the multiple times he tiptoed around his alcoholic father splayed out in a stupor on the floor. His sacrilege of the blessed charge of parenting could also be recalled by seeing the urine-submerged crucifix of Andres Serrano's *Piss Christ*. In this way, by participation an art seeker can experience even in a chaotic or repellent work of art the power to redeem inner darkness or reactivate long-suppressed hope and faith.

The third characteristic of contemporary art that makes it especially useful for art healing is its eschewal of technical virtuosity, which emphasizes and enhances ambiguity. The more ambiguity a work reflects, the more opportunities there may be to project onto it your own ideas to catalyze healing. The ambiguity in art allows you to fill in the unknowns with information from your own psyche. This process also occurs with regard to projective tests. For example, the ambiguity present in the

Thematic Apperception Test illustrations is crucial for eliciting and interpreting patients' responses to images that may be responsible for the "resultant story that indicates inner needs."[31] Like the third grade project in which students pick a picture and tell a tale to stimulate creativity, art seekers can focus on artworks to do much the same thing. For example, Mark Greenwold's paintings[32] invite the viewer to study caricatures of his friends and family members with their disembodied heads floating in the abstract interior spaces of a household. Further, the photographic works of Philip-Lorca diCorcia give little choice but to invest in figuring out the situations presented by the artist, in which alienated people are depicted within confined areas, with few objects as clues to their life circumstances. In identifying with the people (prostitutes, pole dancers, and folks on the street), even if they differ markedly from those in your own life, you can perhaps make better sense of some inner struggle—such as being alienated from yourself and others.

In fact, the level of ambiguity that occurs in abstract art can actually free the viewer from the shackles of verisimilitude to enter the work through what you might imagine as large pores. For example, the central gallery of Barcelona's Fundació Antoni Tàpies features a blank canvas with two mounds of dunglike material that exudes personal freedom, as do Tàpies's other large works created by spontaneously rubbing, scratching, painting, and tossing grit onto a canvas. Such works of dense symbolization and ambiguous meaning lend themselves well to use by art seekers for identification and resolution of personal conflicts and problems.

Partially abstract works, on the other hand, are especially effective for experiencing the benefits of both abstract and representational art, providing an opportunity for healing through both the aesthetic and symbolic functions. In any abstract-representational work, consider the lines and irregular shapes first, allowing thoughts and feelings to emerge. Doing this results in a kind of meditation on physical form, as you inhale the lines, exhale the irregular shapes, and let your mind wander, observing the psychic material emerging from a graphic emptiness.

Rooftop—Sherman Street IV, 2008, Ling-Wen Tsai

Examples of abstract-representational works that encourage extensive self-reflection are artist Ling-Wen Tsai's stunning digital photographs of dark, snow-encrusted rooftops with small pools of reflective standing water, such as *Rooftop—Sherman Street IV*, 2008.[33] The thin layers of water and snow form fields of color that divide the large photographic print into sections. Snow creates a silver-gray ground with what appear to be infrequent bits of dead leaves or other tree matter lying on the surface. Water, on the other hand, creates vast areas of reflected color, like the dominating rust-colored field in the upper left, apparently reflecting the identically colored shingles of an adjacent building. While the work is mostly abstract, there are also areas with recognizable forms, such as house windows reflected in a puddle, so you can alternate between submersion in abstraction and contemplation of representational objects. The clarity of reflected images suggests that water, in its ability to capture objects by reflection, is like a camera, and the viewer is mesmerized by the result as the first viewers of photographs must have been. As a result, *Rooftop—Sherman Street IV* and the darker, even more abstract *Rooftop—High Street I* [34] are particularly well suited for self-reflection.

The fourth characteristic of contemporary art that makes it especially suitable for art healing is its frequent replication of mass media images. As such, it can provide a familiar environment of mass media references and glossy images, much as the modern world saturated with advertising and media communications like TV and the Internet. Such artwork can confront the viewer with images that may be hard to understand but are designed to be visually appealing, like eating a steady diet of high-fructose corn syrup–laden candy and soda. The deceptively simple aesthetic quality of images from our daily experience—banner ads on Internet Web sites, ads on the sides of buses, food packaging, clothing labels—provide communication with something inside of us, using a trick of evolution to prey on our susceptibility to surfaces and our eagerness for promises of a better day. But when artists cleverly manipulate the same advertising images they have the potential to give us a reality check on our materialist obsessions and rescue us by throwing us a Butter Rum lifesaver that encourages us to reassess our priorities.

A final characteristic of contemporary art that makes it particularly well suited to art healing is its self-conscious attention to human and cultural diversity. Today's art, uninhibited by arcane cultural prohibitions and other forms of censorship, emphasizes freedom of creative expression,

Rooftop—High Street I, 2007, Ling-Wen Tsai

including of concepts, images, and media, as well as openness to interpretation of meaning. This could take the form of a photographic study of refugees, acts of war, or the oppression of certain people, including women in a society—such as Rania Matar's photographs of the Palestinian refugee camp in Beirut; depiction of the various sexualities or the challenging of gender as a cultural construct; portrayal of contemporary modes of thought and the creative manipulation of the cliché or authoritative voice, as in the conceptual art of Jenny Holzer or Barbara Kruger; or focus on the bizarre, as in the sexual differentiation process-inspired Cremaster videos by Matthew Barney, the small, politically charged cartoon-like graffiti by Dan Petroski, or the monumental Central Park *Gates* by Christo. Openness in creative expression has led some people to question the artistic value of certain artworks. Nobuyoshi Araki's photographs focusing on sadomasochism, Yoshitomo Nara's deceptively simple anime-inspired portraits of children, and Janine Antoni's copper gargoyle atop the Chrysler Building through which she peed, represent the range of works resulting from today's freedom of artistic expression.

For some art seekers, such contemporary works reflecting aspects of modern life can offer a context for their own frenetic inner experiences, while for others noncontemporary art may spark an awareness that aspects of modern life are causing them anxiety and depression. For example, looking at an impressionist landscape like Camille Pissarro's *Landscape at Chaponval* (1880, Musée d'Orsay), portraying a pastoral scene of a woman and her cow on a beautiful day, might make it all too clear what is lacking in your frenzied life—a peaceful space for reflection and renewal. Alternatively, the varied faces of thirty-three fifteenth-century wooden sculptures representing Kannon, the Buddhist deity of compassion, might reveal a long-suppressed need for spirituality in your life in a way that circuit-board–containing devotional wall hangings could not. The greater the variety of art you view, with all its ideas and possibilities for reflection, the greater your chances for self-revelation and healing.

In the following chapters you will learn how the concerns of many different people were transformed by this intimate dance with works by various artists and how you can use the method of art healing for your own healing. Initially, to get a feeling for each function you could go art healing after reading each chapter, exploring art from the viewpoint of a single function fresh in your mind.

As you become a seasoned art seeker, since functions tend to co-occur you will naturally integrate these functions to the point where you use them as opportunities are presented by various kinds of artworks, effortlessly perceiving by which function insights are evoked.

1
Eye Candy for the Soul
THE AESTHETIC FUNCTION

"You will realize that this combination of red-ocher, of green gloomed over by gray, the black streaks surrounding the contours, produces something of the sensation of anguish, called 'noir-rouge,' from which certain of my companions in misfortune frequently suffer."[1]

—Van Gogh, in a letter to Emile Bernard, Saint Remy, December 1889

ONE OF THE FASTEST AND EASIEST WAYS ART SEEKERS CAN GAIN INSIGHTS for self-healing is through the aesthetic function, which involves engaging art through its basic visual qualities, such as color, form, texture, line, structure, and light and shadow. For example, you might at first be taken in by a work's bright colors that make you feel particularly good. As you further reflect, you might discover that the choice of colors, different types of paint, sharp space-piercing surfaces, clever arrangements of glowing artificial light sources, and smooth renderings of objects resonate with your past experiences, current circumstances, or desires. As you continue to absorb the work, you may enter a deeper realm where you recognize in some aspects of the work a self-defeating compulsion or injurious pattern of coping that has long inhibited full self-expression in your life. When a work of art evokes awareness of conflicted feelings about an intimate relationship, or elicits a sense of loss surrounding a frayed parent-child relationship, or holds sway over your mood, or causes the kind of physical sensation such as when hairs stand up to "do the wave" on the back of your neck, or even whispers into your mind's ear a possible way out of a predicament, you have started to experience therapeutic engagement through the aesthetic function.

An example of how focusing on colors, forms, and materials can result in therapeutic engagement and insight are the possible considerations you might have when viewing Guenter A. Werner's *Ballet*.[2] In this work, a minimalist collection of pastel-shaded items, soft-colored paint in jars hang suspended from wires; a thin yellow looped hose containing orange paint sags from the wall; a huge ceramic tile is divided into tones of pink and blue; large plastic buckets half-filled with paint are hooked to the wall in a Ferris-wheel pattern, looking like a large children's watercolor palette. As you engage with the colors, shapes, and composition of the art, you might at first wonder what it must be like to be an infant. Liquid contained in the looped hose might remind you of a heavy diaper, and the oversized pink and blue tile could suggest the classic gender-based hues of newborn babies. From general thoughts and feelings about infancy, you might reflect on more specific ones, such as experiences during the first year of your life. Then you might shift to reflections on a time when you were older and life was more complicated due to specific failings of your parents that left you feeling the kind of desperation that has forced you to overidealize your early childhood. You might then reassess the usefulness of your persistent fantasy of a serene childhood and become aware of how that perspective has kept you blind to the toxic truth of both your childhood and the circumstances of more recent relationships.

The physical qualities of an artwork can not only give you insights into conflicts but also make you aware of your deficits, such as unmet emotional needs. One man, whose relationships with women were based exclusively on shared intellectual interests, found an answer to his problems concerning romance by considering the color in a work of American impressionism, Ernest Lawson's *Garden Landscape*, circa 1915.[3] In the painting, impastoed red flowers the color of thick red lips sit on long stems pointing skyward. The flowers' "juiciness" reminded him of the qualities he yearned for in a partner but was unable to find because he habitually selected them as if choosing a mutual fund. Inspecting the garden scene's colors, which had been created by multiple brushstrokes of different hues, he realized that even though they seemed unfocused when viewed close up, they appeared vibrant and unified when viewed at more of a distance, giving him the sense that romance might work better when allowed to happen without so much control, more the way nature seems to operate.

Attention to a work's texture also might stimulate reflection and insights about life circumstances. Upon examination of seventeenth-century Dutch painter Willem Claesz Heda's *Still Life with Gilt Cup*, 1635,[4] one art seeker found

Still Life with Gilt Cup, 1635, Willem Claesz Heda

himself feeling "real" and "satisfied" for the first time in recent memory. While this work appears to be a realistic rendering of objects on a table, presumably after a feast—including a green glass goblet, a silken tablecloth, intricate gilt cup, pewter plates, and silver tureen—their exquisite textures made this work emotionally evocative for the viewer. Irregularly occurring wrinkles in a bunched-up white tablecloth, decorative dimples in a silver compote viewed from both convex and concave perspectives, the reflection of a gold cup in an adjacent tureen's shiny surface, the thickly stemmed goblet with grip-enhancing bumps, and the ridged birdlike cruet together yielded a visual lusciousness that made the art seeker aware of his hunger for beauty and the enjoyment of simple pleasures in his usually quotidian life. Subsequently, his attention to the painting's details motivated him to learn to savor basic activities of life, such as eating and drinking, as well as other pursuits he loved but habitually deprived himself of, like spending time with his daughter.

In addition to color, form, and texture, the visual elements of line, light, and shadow can also forge a connection to dormant feelings and give a viewer important personal insights. Fiona, whose art healing led her to surrealist Giorgio de Chirico's *Piazza D'Italia (Italian Square)*, 1954, found that she could tap into the anonymity and surrealistic nature of the scene. The painting, looking like what she imagined could be the result of a psychedelic mechanical drawing class, depicted unadorned Italianate colonnades with deep perspective on either side, opening up to a vacuous plaza, except, that is, for a reclining marble sculpture. The sharply drawn lines, the distinct shadows, the outline of the reclining Greek figure,[5] and the presence of two distant anonymous figures emphasized the starkness and emptiness of Fiona's own life, in which she did not have a single friend except the person she employed as her therapist. It was precisely the elements that make this scene so unnerving that, paradoxically, attracted Fiona and provided psychological benefit.

In addition to the surface attributes of art, a work's structure could lead to therapeutic insights. For example, one art seeker, Morgan, while viewing Dennis Oppenheim's *Performance Piece*, 2000,[6] was transfixed by the structure of the outdoor brick chimney that bends back upon itself, creating a knot. While this piece did contain symbolic elements and could be imagined as a large instrument producing perpetual music, suggested by the many bugles embedded within the chimney's base, its structure is what most contributed to Morgan's healing. The chimney with its knot made her more acutely aware of how she shaped her life around chronic intestinal discomfort. To her, *Perfor-*

mance Piece served as an inspiration to push beyond her own limitations by creating things with her hands, and thus to build a better life by emphasizing her specialness as an asset.

A work's construction materials are another means of discovering important insights about yourself, especially when you have the urge to touch an artwork's soft piece of fabric or a primal craving to lick a fur-lined teacup or when you feel reviled at the danger intrinsic to sharp rusted steel shavings intentionally dropped on the gallery floor. When art triggers such feelings, reflecting on their significance within your life circumstances can help you increase awareness. For example, maybe the quality of aqua-tinted translucent plastic organic forms remind you of a pleasant time scuba diving, or perhaps it instead conjures up feelings of horror connected with a traumatic near-drowning experience. One woman associated the material of an artwork with the scratchy beard of her mother's boyfriend, whom she had seduced.

Another basic visual quality, projected light, as in a video or multimedia installation, can stimulate insight by providing an emotionally evocative visual environment. One young man, Simon, quelled his anxiety by focusing intently on Tim White-Sobieski's *New York Suite*, 2005.[7] The quality of the light emanating from this work changes periodically from something resembling cool moonlight to something resembling hot-white daylight. Tim White-Sobieski's Web site describes the work as follows: "Colored squares and lines in 'Mondrian style' have been recreated in *New York Suite*. Sheer, bright lavender and dark plum with thin golden stripes, this video animates a sensual effect of a sunset or dawn. As the New York sunset disappears, its patterns feature a plaid motif in sophisticated shades of blue, violet and gold."[8] When experiencing this work, Simon reflected on his chronic emotional distress stemming from family circumstances. His father was volatile, demanding, and often shamed Simon when he would make trivial mistakes, such as dropping a screwdriver while helping his father in the garage. To combat his anxiety, Simon would imagine his father being killed while standing, as he often did, on a ladder with a few inches of water on the floor in the perennially flooded cellar. Not wanting to become like his father, whom he regarded as a crass philistine, Simon aspired to a career in the upper echelon of public social work.

Simon described his experience of viewing *New York Suite* in the following way: "I lost myself, and the shapes and colors bled backwards into my brain as if connected by Bluetooth, wirelessly. I could almost feel a tingle under my scalp as I scanned the morphing squares and lines like some bar code being registered into the cash register." Initially the quality of the light stimulation seemed to have a calming effect like that of a Yule log burning in a fireplace, offering a relaxing continuity. Yet this sea of undulating lights led to haunting flashbacks that revealed harrowing feelings, popping to the surface like buoyant life preservers. This provided a chance for the art seeker to allow gnawing feelings to lose their tenacious hold over him by taking refuge in a healing powerlessness that ensued from a kind of visual hypnosis. Engulfing, eye-catching patterns of light distracted him from his anxiety, and deflated overpowering fantasies involving electrocution and patricide, making Simon aware of his desire to live without pressure and angst. Simon's sensations occurred because piercing or flickering lights usually give a feeling of powerlessness that a person with anxiety can use beneficially to distract them from a neurotic looping of thoughts so they can experience more peace,[9] an effect that can also be experienced by strolling through a fluorescent light installation or a tunnel of multicolored neon like at Chicago's O'Hare Airport.

In addition to creating a mood-changing environment, an artwork's light might prompt an art seeker to project images onto it, providing clues to solving inner struggles. For example, Ken Jacobs's *Celestial Subway Lines/Salvaging Noise*, 2005,[10] with its black-and-white rotational landscape, could provide opportunities for quelling anxieties. One art seeker, Bill, who was reclusive, swallowed sedatives like they were M&Ms, was hooked on marijuana, had anxiety that caused him to sweat, and saw projected onto the artwork objects that illuminated his concerns. He said of his light show experience: "Your brain wants to hold on to an image, but then it disappears and the picture returns to you like a boomerang." Even though the complexity of undulating forms made it difficult for Bill to recognize what he was watching, when he zoned out he was able to see the shape of what he thought was a wolf or a human profile. The hallucinatory images he saw—the Wheaties man and wolf's face—were not just random illusions but represented childhood comforts and fears, causing him to remark, "I realized only I saw a profile from a cereal box, or a wolf's face, whereas no one else watching this probably saw these same objects." The projected images gave Bill a kind of *This Is Your Life* experience, opening doors to self-discovery. He recalled how, in childhood, he had associated the Wheaties man with fear of abandonment because his parents had had a horrible fight one morning while he had been eating breakfast. When Bill practiced this process more, as he repeatedly watched the video he purposely instructed himself to relax and "get into it," even though he was ordinarily prone to nausea, saying, "I told myself I would emerge with greater creativity, enjoy my life more, be more open to new ideas, and more overtly value people I care about—my kids and their mother." Bill appreciated that without the use of psychedelic drugs, the art seemed to tattoo something important on his cortex, as if he were a shaman reading something from ephemeral images while looking into flames. This process helped him quell his childhood anxieties about abandonment and, at the same time, rescued him from his quotidian life by transporting him to a zone of creativity and mystery by the devices of abstraction and ambiguity.

A final benefit of the aesthetic function in art healing is the general uplifting feeling that can be evoked by the materials and construction of magnificent works of art, such as Nick Cave's colorful and intricately detailed costumes in *Recent Soundsuits*, 2009.[11] This artwork features costumes of tall, pointed or flat contiguous headpieces with only a few exposed heels of smoky black manikins, all standing on one of two foot-high platforms resembling fashion runways. On one platform are six figures facing different directions, all with fuzzy, wildly dyed synthetic hair. On a U-shaped platform stand seventeen other figures, also elaborately costumed. Some hold their arms in back of them in a seem-

Recent Soundsuits, 2009, Nick Cave
Photo: James Prinz

ingly human pose. One displays cotton-candy pink, round patches within a background of black and brown hair. Another has what seems like a tall chef's hat with long stripes in lime green, bright purple, pink, cream, red, orange, and blue. Many figures have embroidered stockings on the feet. A few have a metal scaffold hung over the shoulders as a headpiece supporting multiple ceramic painted-bird figurines like the kind nursing home residents paint and hand off to staff members for glazing. Owls, flowers, patches, and chains of beads are draped around the metallic scaffold, forming a kitschy bush.

Other costumes include cages in which are suspended metal flowers extending upward by several feet. Still other costumes have hundreds of buttons and thousands of sequins in different shades of purples, greens, yellows, and light blue in spiral patterns with radiating spikes. One costume is like a tricked-out wedding dress with fake diamonds, variegated tiny pearly balls, and shiny plastic tubes, the patterns looking like feathers and wings, starbursts, crunchy granola, and the end result of a tornado in a button factory. Another costume has triangular areas of single-color sequins of green, purple, blue, and pink interrupted by alternating eel-shaped streams of dark- and aqua-blue sequins, while on the back are tiny mirrors embedded in the stitching and floral designs, patterns within patterns that are like the stuff of fractal geometry discoverer Benoit Mandelbrot's dreams.

The aspects of this work combine to evoke in the art seeker the gleeful stimulation a child experiences when faced with fascinating colors, textures, and shapes. The various features could be reminiscent of carnival revelers, Easter Island monoliths, Jim Henson's Muppets, *Star Wars'* Chewbacca, tie-dyed Holstein cows, or parts in a Dr. Seuss-inspired acid trip. In addition to gaining possible insights through associations with the structure and other physical traits of the work, because of its complexity an art seeker might also reflect on the labor required to produce it, and thus, by extension, their own motivation in life or lack thereof.

Further, the work might prompt reflections on various cultures since it projects a feeling of multicultural celebration with numerous cultural references suggested by the characteristics of costumes and the ambiguity of their shapes and sizes. Thus, an art seeker might take comfort in how the work seems to reflect both universality and the vitality and diversity of life. A consideration of such ideas demonstrates how the aesthetic function overlaps with the symbolic function, which prompts art seekers to ponder how images and objects in artworks reflect circumstances in their own lives.

2

What It All Means
THE SYMBOLIC FUNCTION

"I can't make a distinction between emotion and intellect, but this has something to do with my use of iconography. When I use a skull, it's not because it exists in Bellini or El Greco, but because it makes a certain emotional sense when it's painted in a certain work. That means it has a certain relation to life, expresses a certain attitude or outlook. I think of my paintings as effecting an attitude which makes life livable for someone else."[1]

—Julian Schnabel, interviewed by Daniel Kuspit, November 1987

THE SYMBOLIC FUNCTION INVOLVES MAKING ASSOCIATIONS BETWEEN OBJECTS or images in an artwork and aspects of an art seeker's inner life, such as conflicts, cognitive or emotional patterns, or past memories that trigger insights into current problems. Although German philosopher Immanuel Kant reasoned it was impossible to fully experience things themselves with our limited sensory capacity,[2] artworks can bring us close to knowing them by the quality with which they are rendered, their emotional impact on us, and their incorporation of potentially symbolic objects. Given the fact that most artworks have at least some recognizable objects from everyday life or evocative images, they can quickly lead to self-reflection and insightful realizations. Maybe the ghostly outline of dysmorphic toes reminds you of a critical figure in your childhood; or perhaps a graffitied chubby doll's head gives you a sense of where you were emotionally at a given point in time. Or maybe a fake windmill at a miniature golf course or a nose can readily suggest important life events or pivotal moments in your personal development, such as a resort vacation just before your father died or your busybody aunt who refuses to keep her nose out of your business.

Some works might evoke a range of memories. For example, when viewing Takashi Murakami's colorful *Jellyfish Eyes*, 2001,[3] you might move from memories of your wall-eyed brother to a creepy feeling you had once as your uncle showed you flip books of a woman giving head to a guy in uniform as you played pinball together in a basement containing broken bits of coral from someone's vacation or even happily beachcombing on the seashore during a family vacation.

Untitled, 2005, M. Ho

Similarly, an image of a knife dangling over a surface supporting two tomatoes might spark recall of a wide variety of experiences depending on other colors or shapes surrounding it, such as a stint in culinary school, a half-brother who once threatened to stab you, a sharp-tongued aunt who assumed a maternal role when your mother was ill, your own tendency to cut through bullshit and get answers from your employees, or how you cut yourself off from long-term relationships due to a fear of being smothered.

Moreover, holding on to visual pleasure even when you are viewing something disturbing or that evokes a core issue facilitates deeper reflection and additional insights. For example, looking at artist M. Ho's *Untitled*, 2005,[4] which obscures depressing war-related text on the front page of the *New York Times* with images of flowers, may evoke reverie of a peaceful time after a brother returned from service in the military, despite the fact that you have been active in many antiwar protests.

An example of the symbolic function's capacity to induce memory and stimulate self-reflection is the experience that an art seeker, Mark, had while interacting with Marc Trujillo's *1052 West Burbank Boulevard*, 2006,[5] a large painting that depicts a perspective from inside an open-air entrance to a big-box wholesale outlet such as Sam's Club or Costco at dusk. It caused Mark, a general contractor, to review his life since high school. The no-frills, industrial slab construction of the structure triggered memories of phases in his life when he had various attitudes and was involved in relationships associated with construction projects. Gradually his reflection became more focused on specific issues he was currently facing. The large size of the prison-like space, its relationship with the darker adjacent parking lot, and the way the space dwarfs its inhabitants, who eat snacks at red picnic tables that reflect unnatural fluorescent light, were surreal key elements that caused him to assess his unhappy relationship with a girlfriend of seven years. Each figure and item evoked some response to their recent life together: the metal carts overfilled with eight-packs of paper towels made him think about how she always purchased too much as a way to deal with insecurity; the

1052 West Burbank Boulevard, 2006, Marc Trujillo

pictures of cheap foods above the order window made him aware of her unrefined palate; the red garbage cans caused him to conclude that she was a slob; the people in isolation like directionless zombies made him realize they were so disconnected it seemed ridiculous that they had lived to-gether for so many years. Mark's feelings of pain, loneliness, boredom, and powerlessness triggered by the painting gave him clear insights into why his relationship with his girlfriend was undermining his potential for a fulfilling life.

Along with inducing thoughts and memories, objects or images in artworks can also provide a vehicle for guiding your inner self. One art seeker, Candace, lost herself in some of the images in Masaru Tatsuki's *Decotora*, or *Japanese Art Truck Scene*, 1998–2007,[6] which caused her to experience something like visual meditation. Ironically, her inability to decipher one particularly complex image helped her use it therapeutically. Even after learning from gallery staff that the image was of many brightly illuminated trucks lined up together, she could see only what appeared to be a room filled with bizarre lights, like the interior of a casino with infinity mirrors. Being blind to what the image actually represented helped her use what she did see as a visual guide to aspects of her inner self.

Where projected light might provide a meditative sensory environment, text in art or art that uses text as its form might speak more directly to a traumatic experience and facilitate healing. One art seeker, Tonya, gained insights into her traumatic experiences by viewing Jenny Holzer's *BAR*, 2008[7]— an appropriation of U.S. military autopsy reports, with seven curved, double-sided LED signs in red, white, and blue, that read, in part:

{AUTOPSY REPORT ME03-504} {XXXXX} {OPINION} {XXXXX}, AN IRAQI NATIONAL, DIED WHILE DETAINED AT THE ABU GHRAIB PRISON WHERE HE WAS HELD FOR IN-TERROGATIONS BY GOVERNMENT AGENCIES. ACCORDING TO AN INVESTIGATIVE REPORT, MR. {XXXXX} WAS CAPTURED BY NAVY SEAL TEAM #7 AND RESISTED AP-PREHENSION. EXTERNAL INJURIES ARE CONSISTENT WITH INJURIES SUSTAINED DUR-ING APPREHENSION. LIGATURE INJURIES ARE PRESENT ON THE WRISTS AND ANKLES. FRACTURES OF THE RIBS AND A CONTUSION OF THE LEFT LUNG IMPLY SIGNIFICANT BLUNT FORCE INJURIES OF THE THORAX AND LIKELY RESULTED IN IMPAIRED RESPIRA-

TION. ACCORDING TO INVESTIGATING AGENTS, INTERVIEWS TAKEN FROM INDIVIDU-ALS PRESENT AT THE PRISON DURING THE INTERROGATION INDICATE THAT A HOOD MADE OF SYNTHETIC MATERIAL WAS PLACED OVER THE HEAD AND NECK OF THE DETAINEE. THIS LIKELY RESULTED IN FURTHER COMPROMISE OF EFFECTIVE RESPIRA-TION. MR. {XXXXX} WAS NOT UNDER THE INFLUENCE OF DRUGS OF ABUSE OR ETHA-NOL AT THE TIME OF DEATH. THE CAUSE OF DEATH IS BLUNT FORCE INJURIES OF THE TORSO COMPLICATED BY COMPROMISED RESPIRATION. THE MANNER OF DEATH IS HOMICIDE...

Tonya felt as if the text scrolling by in bright lights resonated with childhood torture that she had not fully acknowledged. She remembered how her authoritarian father and mean stepbrothers used to gang up on her and how she suffered abuse while her mother, also a victim of abuse and a Valium addict, looked the other way. Later in life, Tonya had felt she could move beyond painful family memo-ries only by allowing herself to be dominated by other forces, such as unhealthy personal relationships. But now after years of self-injurious behavior, serial bad relationships, and a bout with alcoholism, she was ready to stop seeking respect from those who disrespected her and acknowledge her habitual role as victim.

Even though the words and phrases of *BAR* were a comment about torture and Abu Ghraib, Tonya identified with the images of the abuse expressed. And she felt a kinship with the artist, who, she presumed, understood the nature of abuse on a fundamental level. Moreover, knowing that a female artist had created the work—rather than a male artist who might have made her recall the abuse by the men in her family—helped Tonya surrender to the experience to effect healing.

Considering a work's layers, either structural or thematic, plays a central role in helping to break down the mind's defenses to obtain insights about core issues. Like your own psyche, a work of art is

Greed, 2008, Kelly Jo Shows

both a unified whole and also consists of layers that when peeled away may result in discovery of what is at the core. This process of revelation can yield valuable information about essences, like undressing to become naked and vulnerable. Layers as a theme in artworks might suggest past, present, and future; release and renewal; or changes of identity. In two examples by Polish artist Pawel Althamer, *Self-Portrait As a Business Man*, 2002–04 and *Self-Portrait*, 1994,[8] a man's

trappings of quotidian life are either left on the floor (in the former) or sealed in plastic, appearing like an oversized garment bag (in the latter), as if the person had disrobed—left all of his identification, currency, clothes, and even a swath of hair behind—and gone skinny dipping to swim to a new way of living. When viewing this work, an art seeker might ponder the identity, motivation, and fate of the person. Then these reflections could be an impetus for self-examination regarding the authentic self apart from cultural restrictions or social personas.

The more you uncover layers of an artwork, the more you might reveal yourself. One art seeker, Devon, a manufacturing sales representative, habitually defined his identity by the clothes he wore, his position in the hierarchy, and the kind of car he drove. But when looking at Kelly Jo Shows's *Greed*, 2008,[9] Devon found that as he visually peeled away the layers of the work he could effect a parallel process in himself to become more aware of his authentic self. The work is comprised of a stop sign fixed to a backing, turning the work into a three-dimensional octagonal box. Below the letters there is a small rectangular hole big enough to allow a person to reach a hand partway in. One layer consists of three small channels of broken glass with sharp shards pointing up as though guarding the opening. The next layer is made of a thick roll of dollar bills that dangle from a string. Finally, there is a mirror behind the glass and bills. The more Devon considered each of the work's layers, the more he could see his own essence, which, he discovered, lacked much substance. He realized he didn't know who he was and that he spent all his time, apart from the demands of making a living, superficially engaged—parroting AM radio talking points, flaunting good looks, and employing savvy sales tricks such as spilling vanilla extract to aromatically seduce clients. While examining the layers of this work more closely, he saw the stop sign as his own struggle with acting civilly, and his tendency to bend the rules for personal profit. The channels of broken glass felt to Devon like the threat of exposure and ruin from his aggressive drive for financial rewards. Devon interpreted the roll of dollar bills dangling from a string as reflecting his raison d'être—moneymaking—and his insatiable desire for more money at the expense of his humanity. Finally, Devon saw the small mirror behind the glass and the bills as his self-interest and concern with appearance and surface features. The process of simultaneously peeling away layers of the work and of his own psyche provided Devon the insights necessary to nurture his soul and begin living a less superficial and more satisfying life.

The symbolic function also helped one woman intensify an intentional recollection of emotional pain for healing. Sheila, a thirty-four-year-old single administrative assistant with a history of bulimia and compulsive shopping, emotionally healed herself by interacting with works of contemporary pop artist Kenny Scharf at a New York gallery.[10] Sheila's consideration of the large works, with their interplay of oil paint, acrylics, and silkscreen ink, stimulated her reconnection to a time when symptoms of her eating disorder first emerged. When faced with a large jar of Tang floating in a glitter-specked outer space (*Tang*, 2007), she flashed back to scenes from her adolescence at home binging at night on Mallowmars and Breyers Ice Cream, followed by feelings of shame and self-loathing that lasted

Tang, 2007, Kenny Scharf

until she retreated to the bathroom to purge the food and ill feelings, splattering the sink so it looked like a Jackson Pollock–style action painting. In this way, she gained insights about how her behavior stemmed from her lonely and empty home environment. Like the void of Scharf's glitter-specked outer space, made doubly empty by the false promise of Tang's good nutrition, Sheila's home life had been cold and impersonal, where the warmth she craved came primarily from steaming Lean Cuisine entrees fresh from the microwave. On the odd occasion

of a sit-down dinner, she could not bear to eat in front of family members, experiencing physical pain, inability to breathe, and sweating when she watched others eat.

Sheila had expressed her emptiness through three pastimes: buying, eating, and competing with her mother. Although Sheila had fallen into a binge-and-purge pattern before college, on campus her electrolytes became so out of whack that she frequently couldn't function, prompting multiple emergency room visits and finally getting the attention of her distracted parents. After entering a residential program for eating disorders, Sheila's bulimia stabilized, but she then developed a pathological relationship with shopping, not unlike her mother's unrestrained consumption. As a symbol for her uncontrollable impulse to shop, she lined up her many shoes in the hallway of her dorm until the fire inspectors took issue with the clutter. Soon shopping became a daily obsession, resulting in painful accumulations of credit card debt intermittently forgiven by her guilt-stricken father, on whom she relied for financial help.

Other works appearing in Scharf's catalog relating to fast food evoked similar responses in Sheila. One work, *Chips Galore, aka Chip, Chip, Hooray! Aka Mother Chip aka Where the Chips May Fall aka Joy,* 2007, created in oil, acrylic, and silkscreen ink on linen, provided the most access to her world of consumption. She stated:

> I could feel myself curling up inside my head simply by the way [the painting] looked and appealed to me. The many bits of products and people brought me immediately to the good feelings generated when I went food shopping with my mother. I remember being enthralled with foods and the glossy packaging and positive associations connected with a handy TV dinner, which I would eat in front of the TV. I imagine my own mother when I look at the retro 1950s-style mother spilling out Wise potato chips from a bag as she floats in the right upper corner with eyes closed and a bright white smile, the chips floating everywhere across the huge linen

Chips Galore, aka Chip, Chip, Hooray! Aka Mother Chip aka Where the Chips May Fall aka Joy, 2007, Kenny Scharf

> canvas as if in zero gravity. And I see myself in the girl with one eye closed taking a chip in one hand while holding a cup in the other.

The visual cacophony of these and other acrylic-painted products (Sony Trinitron television set, Velveeta cheese box, Johnson & Johnson cotton balls, Zest deodorant soap, Blue Bonnet margarine) in *Chips Galore* stimulated Sheila's search for answers to her inner conflicts. She could identify with the little girl who in each

Cosmic Crude, 2007, Kenny Scharf

hand held a symbol of her attempts to heal her emotional wounds: a chip representing eating comfort food and a cup signifying the attempt to quench thirst for love and affection. She realized how both food and shopping had falsely promised satisfaction throughout her life.

Sheila was further prompted to search for clues to the motivations behind her behavior by viewing the alluringly bright forms of lipstick (*Cosmic Crude*, 2007), a juicy steak (*Great to Meet Shoe*, 2007), Kraft parmesan cheese (*One Good Thing Leads to Another*, 2007), an overflowing

Ketchup bottle (*Ketchup*, 2006), and fried chicken legs that become projectiles radiating outward into space (*Chickendala*, 2007). After more reflection about the relationship between these images and her behavior, she realized she could not have grown up as she did, in an environment of coldness and emptiness, without any compensatory consequence, and that her binging, purging, and overconsumption had developed around attempts to satisfy her deep craving for love and affection from her family.

As a result of observing the artworks, Sheila saw that the layers of paint and images suggested gaining control over attractions and impulses. She realized that she no longer needed to slavishly indulge her momentary desires by binging or shopping but could learn to allow herself to enjoy life's pleasures in less self-destructive ways. Sheila's conclusion was that satisfaction of desire in itself was not ruining her life, and the unsatisfactory way she coped with her inner emptiness was the problem. Viewing the food items presented in fascinating colors and textures made her understand she could indulge inner desires

Great to Meet Shoe, 2007, Kenny Scharf

One Good Thing Leads to Another, 2007, Kenny Scharf

aesthetically, rather than by eating and shopping to shield against pain. Sheila's realization was amplified by the fact that she now saw she could make "art" in her life with the glossy packaging that used to hold her under its spell if she acknowledged its superficiality and did not rely on it to compensate for her inner emptiness and thus learn to enjoy life's pleasures in new, more fulfilling ways.

When an art seeker considers so many works with intense visual qualities, it is helpful to allow them to coalesce into a single symbol that sums up the experience and the reflection on personal issues. For example, Sheila's observations and reflections coalesced into a symbol of the chocolate-iced donut with sparkles in Scharf's *Chocolate Donut in Space*, 2007,[11] which seems to spin and glis-

Ketchup, 2006, Kenny Scharf

ten in outer space like an edible black hole. For Sheila, it simultaneously symbolized the eating disorder and the inner emptiness that threatened her health and happiness, as well as what she needed to do to improve her life—view her desires more objectively without relinquishing them altogether. As she put it: "I stare at the big donut and imagine myself running in circles around and around the donut as it spins in space, like I'm running laps at the gym. But I know that I must also take a bite from the donut from time to time." To top off her experience reflecting on the art, as she left the gallery space Sheila met Kenny Scharf and his crew, who were dressed for an art event, in faux astronaut gear, and riding on the golf cart sculpture *Carzy Roy-Al* around the streets of Chelsea. He offered passersby, including Sheila, a jelly donut, which she swallowed gleefully, regarding it as both a way to remind herself in the future to indulge inner desires aesthetically and not to use food as a way to avoid pain. An art seeker can benefit additionally by taking another once-around the gallery to search for a similar encompassing pattern, image, or theme that sums up the most salient personal aspects of the day's art healing.

Beyond catalyzing personal insights, images or text in art may expand an art seeker's perspective on cultural contexts that impact their life. Just as Scharf's eye-catching images gave Sheila an art seeker's insights about her consumptive behaviors, a layer of stamped-out text broadened her view of her situation as an American woman in a consumer-driven capitalist society. In Scharf's works, the swirls of bright colors and text written in different languages made her increasingly aware of how she was seduced daily by advertising and packaging, as if she were a fish being hooked by a lure, whether the fantasy of a beautiful life or the promise of glamour to be found at a mall department store makeup counter. She saw

Chickendala, 2007, Kenny Scharf

Chocolate Donut in Space, 2007, Kenny Scharf

clearly how she had to confront aspects of a consumer society daily—in the mail, on the Internet, near storefronts, on television, in magazines, or on billboards or posters. Seeing her personal struggles with consumption in the larger context of society's consumerism provided a broader perspective on how society had made it easier for her to be seduced by food and consumer goods to cover up her emotional problems.

As exemplified by Sheila's experience, the symbolic function can allow art seekers to see themselves in a cultural mirror that might clarify the challenges they face by having to function in a frenetic world dominated by telecommunications and lack of leisure, often with a cell phone seeming to grow out of an ear, chained to desks, and pushing virtual paper around in a cyber-environment. Such art has the potential to speak to a population doing most of their living within Wal-Marts, office parks, and ubiquitous fast-food joints that James Howard Kunstler cheekily refers to as "fry pits."[12] When art seekers recognize the self in a cultural mirror provided by art, they acquire the potential to broaden their perspective on how their personal issues may be influenced by cultural phenomena.

Art healing's symbolic function includes discovering and relating to artistic depictions of doppelgängers, or "doubles," that facilitate self-evaluation as if looking through a window at the self in a parallel world. Looking for a doppelgänger in artworks takes seeing aspects of the self in art to a higher level. Occurring throughout the history of artistic creation, the device of doppelgängers is a useful means of facilitating a deeper psychological reading of an individual's core issues within the psyche. In searching for doppelgängers in art, you don't just relate to a figure, idea, or image in the art for personal insight but parts of or an entire artwork can become a stand-in for you and the way you live. This aspect of art healing parallels Carl Jung's idea that all figures in a dream in one way or another represent different parts of the dreamer's self.

One art seeker, Mike, recognized his double when viewing photographs by Gregory Crewdson from the 1996–97 *Hover* series,[13] which depicts painstakingly choreographed ambiguous narrative scenes featuring suburbanites. The photograph that most drew Mike shows a man laying down sod in the middle of a street lined with Levitt-style ranch houses. In the places where he labors, once clean, messes are soon made, so he has to keep repeating this work. A police car's door is open, and an officer stands in the street—but from where he is standing he would not be able to see the man bent over laying down rectangles of sod on the cement street. A sprinkler from one house waters the street's new lawn, while onlookers that seem like zombies watch. Mike drew a parallel between the people in the Crewdson work and his daily life, especially his job preparing apartments for low-income tenants, which required him to wander to enigmatic dead-ends of planned developments devoid of hope. He observed, "I feel like my life is this street. It might look comfortable, but something's not right." He identified with the man's futile efforts, as if doing something "totally nuts, having to start from scratch the next day." Reflecting on the man as his double, Mike saw himself as working in an unfulfilling job and repeatedly unable to successfully heal troubled relationships with women and put down roots. Further, Mike viewed his situation as parallel to that of one of the zombie-like onlookers, who seemed to reflect social isolation and fear-based immobilization. Ultimately, Mike identified with not only individual figures in the work but the entirety of it, saying, "I'm not just the nut laying down sod in the middle of the road. I'm also the zombie-like onlookers, the dazed cop stuck in his tracks, and even the isolated dead-end road." Mike's viewpoint from this elevated angle offered him perspective on his life circumstances similar to that gained during a psychotherapeutic process.

By seeing their double in artworks, art seekers can not only get a broader perspective on their life circumstances but recognize negative attitudes and behaviors and gain insights about how to substitute positive ones. One art seeker, Ira, an office worker, found his double in Andrew Leonard's curious installation entitled *Idol,* at the Bromfield Gallery in Boston.[14] Seeing the primitive man who is a subject of the artwork as his double helped Ira reestablish a connection with the earth as the source of humanity's development. The installation's centerpiece is three old TV sets perched atop short columns of cinder blocks. Opposite these columns sits a six-foot wall made of stacked cinder blocks attached with a steel chain to the gallery and with a brown leaf stuck on the upper right side. The blocks have chipped edges, from what appears to be dirt thrown on them and scattered on the floor. On the gallery wall, a black scribbled pattern seems to emanate from a drawing of a minimalist house. One of the three TV monitors shows a man wearing a black mask with a white toga over his shins and forearms slowly dragging four cinder blocks attached to a chain through the woods on a wide road, against background images of farm silos and a female figure with wings, a smaller figure with wings, and a tall male figure with wings, reminiscent of a fertility symbol. On the center monitor is the image of a man wearing a black mask and building a cinder block wall at the edge of the woods. The third monitor shows a man punching cinder blocks rhythmically with both fists, sounding like a heartbeat.

Looking at this work, Ira saw an expression of humankind's ancestry and connection to the earth. He noted how the sounds accompanying the imagery resembled those of the basic functioning of human minds and bodies, harkening back to an embryonic stage when a baby hears muffled tones in the mother's uterus. Lulled into a primitive state of being, Ira felt himself tap into something primal and observed, "I feel as if I want to get out from behind the artificial glow of my computer screen and run around in the woods, make a lean-to . . . I want to live by acting, doing, breathing, and being in nature. I want to step off the treadmill of my current life and use my body to achieve practical ends. When I'm on my computer, I'm hungry for something physical. Yet my tendency has been that whenever I get a minute to myself after a long day at the office, I repeat the very actions I want to run away from—like checking my e-mail! Life beckons, but I'm so programmed to do my job that I naturally extend that into my few precious hours of personal time. . . . Looking at the artwork, I see my double holding out a hairy arm to me as I grab it for life."

Despite the potential computers have for separating us from our essential selves, they can also be a good source of psychologically useful art for art seekers. Art specifically created for the Internet can activate the symbolic function and offer possibilities for discovering doppelgängers, thereby initiating personal insights for self-healing. In the same way art seekers can see their doppelgängers mirrored in various other forms of art, such as pre-Columbian and contemporary African figurines, they might also discover their double on a computer screen. The clickable double can even provide the art seeker with additional options for interaction, ultimately yielding freedom. One piece of so-called net art by artist Nicolas Clauss, titled *La Poupee*, 2005[15] appealed to a young woman, Tonya. So shy she would not dare change her hairstyle lest others make comments, she responded well to images of a doll's face caught within a transparent squat glass jar, apparently manipulating its hair with its plastic hands. Tonya felt that the doll was her double, reflecting her social anxiety—an avatar, but quite different from the one she had created in the virtual parallel universe of Second Life or the more stripped-down version she used when playing with her brother on the Wii. Looking at the doll's head, with its one dark brown eye, Tonya said, "I feel caught behind my longish hair, stuck in my own jar. Caught in the screen, I disappear and become just an eye." By studying her double, she saw another way out of the subterranean realm of her boredom and lack of self-esteem besides only using YouTube as her periscope in life. Ultimately, such realizations about the problematic aspects of her life helped Tonya better integrate her outer and inner worlds.

A final aspect of the symbolic function involves bizarre imagery and metaphorical titles that create a dreamlike condition in the art seeker similar to the intuitive understanding a

La Poupee, 2005, Nicolas Clauss

dreamer can have upon waking and sensing the essence of a certain person before consciously deciphering the contents of the dream or sensing the essence of a person after their death or disappearance from the individual's life. Mark Greenwold's works offer such experiences of dreamlike presences. Greenwold's *All Joy Gone (For Marvin)*, 2000-01, *A Moment of True Feeling*, 2004–05, *The Risk of Existence*, 1997, *The Excited Self*, 2005–06, *Why Not Say What Happened*, 2003–04, and *The Need to Understand*, 2002–03[16] are small works of complex, funny, bizarre, dreamlike scenes on wooden panels. Al-

All Joy Gone (For Marvin), 2000-01, Mark Greenwold

person's aura. Other unusual elements contribute to the sense of being in a dream or having a hallucinatory experience like in *Alice in Wonderland*: a stunned cat with one raised paw; a large sniffing rat; a bitten pear resting on the floor; a disproportionately sized man and woman wearing identical yellow housedresses, he levitating toward the ceiling and she bending forward; and a bespectacled woman with her hand made into a fist. Given the uncertainty of meaning, the work's title might allude to the inscrutability of the specific or, more generally, the need to grasp the essence of people or life. Like the way one might reflect on elements in a dream, art seekers

though they are somewhat inscrutable because of metaphorical titles, lack of consistent perspective, composite human-animal figures, areas of abstraction, and blatant disregard for the law of gravity, the surreal human elements offer art seekers tools for studying the psychology of people, perhaps leading to a better understanding of relationships in the art seeker's life. For example, above each human figure's head in *The Need to Understand* floats a colorful pattern that could be imagined as a physical record of the

A Moment of True Feeling, 2004-05, Mark Greenwold

The Risk of Existence, 1997, Mark Greenwold

The Excited Self, 2005-06, Mark Greenwold

can project onto these scenes and imagine what is happening, using the work to better understand scenarios in their own lives. The key to discovering crucial personal insights is for art seekers to consider how the scenes could be symbolic of their own personas or relationships that they may have witnessed or personally experienced.

Another Greenwold work, *You Must Change Your Life,* 2001–02,[17] offers art seekers similar opportunities for understanding their various personas or relationships. In this work, the art seeker views scenes involving small dramas from the perspective of looking through an open glass sliding door. The work depicts a woman holding a barefoot man bent over backwards on her lap; a woman forcing a dagger into the neck of a terrified, bulging-eyed man; a woman who is either blind or suffering with strabismus, wearing a DKNY T-shirt and apparently looking at the slumped-over man; a bald, gray-bearded man, naked except for socks and shoes, seemingly looking at the viewer while a

The Need to Understand, 2002-03, Mark Greenwold

You Must Change Your Life, 2001-02, Mark Greenwold

woman sits behind the bed in the bedroom; and a griffin, a man's head with the body of a large bird, apparently coming out of the top right corner of the same window through which the naked man peers. To an art seeker, such scenes could be symbolic representations of incidents at gatherings of their dysfunctional extended family or events within their own psyches. Such consideration by an art seeker might result in seeing the self as a composite of personas or recognizing unwanted tendencies that need to be altered for a healthier, more productive life. Thus this aspect of the symbolic function might, like Jung says of dreams, aid art seekers in better comprehending disparate parts of themselves.

Clearly the symbolic function offers many ways art seekers can gain personal insights for healthy transformation. As active as art seekers must be to reap the emotional benefits of both the aesthetic and symbolic functions, the participatory involvement in artworks offers even greater potential for personal transformation.

3

You Are the Canvas
THE PARTICIPATORY FUNCTION

"While [my father] was still alive but fading, I was at The Art Institute of Chicago for a
planning meeting about an upcoming show, and I walked into the gallery of fifteenth-century
paintings. There was Dieric Bout's Crying Madonna *all by herself, eyes swollen and red in*
the excruciating detail of the Northern painters' hard-core realism, with tears streaming down
her face. I began sobbing uncontrollably. I couldn't stop. Later I realized what had happened.
A kind of feedback loop had formed, a visceral/emotional circuit had been completed, and
like a mirror, we were both crying—the painting and me. I had fully realized the picture in a
way I never thought about before, and the function of an artwork changed dramatically for
me at that moment. My training in art school was all about responding to artworks in an
intellectual, personal, or cultural way—in other words, as a viewer, not a participant . . . . It
certainly didn't involve a bodily fluid coming uncontrollably out of my eyes!"[1]
—Bill Viola, in conversation with Hans Belting, June 8, 2002

THE PARTICIPATORY FUNCTION OF ART HEALING CONCERNS ACTION BY SOMEONE
other than the artist, most often the viewer, as part of its construction and meaning. For example, such art might ask for a viewer's written or drawn response; call for a viewer to physically
enter a structure; or request a viewer to touch, push, or otherwise manipulate a portion of it.

While the effectiveness of the aesthetic and symbolic functions hinge on the willingness of art
seekers to take an active role by looking, the effectiveness of the participatory function often depends
on the willingness of art seekers to interact with artworks intentionally created to involve other people.

Such interaction, either directly or by identification with a proxy subject, increases the potential for personal change and healing due to the art seeker's scrutiny of their patterns of behavior under specific circumstances. Interacting physically with artworks makes them feel less like art and more like objects in a sociological study that includes an assessment of the art seeker's own behavior. Such art offers a place of play or practice for participants, providing a means of considering different ideas, experiencing different feelings, and achieving different perspectives, forcing you to view yourself in a wider context. Participation in such art becomes at once exposure therapy and a psychological housecleaning. Further, the way the participatory function allows art seekers to act out behaviors is similar to how people participate in dreams, and can, like dreams, provide fertile ground for creative solutions to emotional problems and instill confidence for making important changes in art seekers' lives.

Various artworks can elicit different types of participation, depending on their concepts and construction. One way to understand the potential types of participation is to compare them to the multiple manifestations of movement that can occur when the nervous system is stimulated in a variety of ways. The brain's cerebral cortex might in some instances be the sole catalyst of action. When this part of the brain thinks about movement, it causes electrical impulses that stimulate nerves of the motor tracts and produces movement. Motion can also arise from a reflexive response, such as when a doctor's rubber hammer is used to strike the knee, causing the knee to jerk. Additionally, action may derive from semiconscious flow, like when a hang glider's running gradually turns into gliding.

One type of participation that can be elicited by an artwork is inclusion. Art whose primary focus involves participation by others can have a healing effect by connecting an art seeker with other people for a common purpose, such as alleviating emotional anguish or loneliness, which is also one benefit of group therapy. But in addition to allowing art seekers to be participants in an artwork, this process can also resonate with their core issues and thus potentially provide useful insights for healing.

Self-Portraits of Heterosexual Men (gallery view), 2007, Gabriel Martinez

For example, such art helped one art seeker, Zach, revise unhealthy formative childhood experiences and gain greater confidence in himself. Responding in this way created in Zach a yearning to better understand his sexuality, helping to reverse a tendency toward existential loneliness.

When Zach entered Samson Projects Gallery in Boston to view Gabriel Martinez's *Self-Portraits of Heterosexual Men*, 2007, the art made him feel as if he were walking onto an adult playground. He saw on the gallery walls one hundred photographs of the legs, ankles, and feet of masturbating men in many contorted positions with telltale shiny droplets of semen. The artist had recruited his subjects by placing ads on social networking Web sites, intentionally bypassing gay men and targeting straight men for inclusion to make a point about experiences of manhood. He had set up each man with a camera whose shutter would release with the touch of a remote control button, which the participant was advised to hit as many times as possible at the point of climax. The participants' legs were as var-

Anonymous 2   *Daniel*

ied as the environments surrounding them: strong, hairy, tattooed, veiny, bruised, dirty, young, and old. The different legs were in various positions—some stuck straight out hovering over the floor, others hanging out awkwardly from the side of a car over crabgrass, and still others lying on a radiator next to a pile of broken sheetrock.

Around the feet were incidental objects that added narrative elements to each scene: a blurred image of a cat and a litter box next to a bathtub; sneakers tossed haphazardly and basketball shorts balled up; and a pile of envelopes near a computer chair. Other important elements in each composition were the various surfaces on which the men sat: a black leather chair with telltale drips coursing slowly down its back; a ripped cheap chair with faux leather; computer chairs; a bathtub; a toilet; a radiator bed; a Victorian-type loveseat; a bed; and a camp trunk. This pseudo-sociological study of a cross section of male autoerotic sexuality made Zach both excited and nauseous. Zach observed, "I got mixed feelings as I viewed the work." He found that while interacting with the work he could affirm his masculinity by empathizing with the participants, but the work also conjured up memories that prompted him to reassess his relationships to men.

Eric

Jason

After the initial titillation, Zach experienced a feeling of disappointment when he realized how the legs and toes of many of the subjects were not beautiful, a fact that was at odds with his usual idealization of maleness. On the one hand, Zach thought about all the times he had sought out saunas to gain a feeling of security and warmth in the world of men and, by holding on to a physical connection to them, like a real man himself. *Self-Portraits* made him wonder if he had ever taken an objective look at what real men's bodies look like outside of dimly lit, steamy environs. On the other hand, for perhaps the first time he felt like he didn't have to make himself attractive to inspire the attention of men and be part of the group who had posed for the camera in the height of ecstasy.

Further, Zach conceded that the artworks reopened painful wounds relating to old desires of wanting to be exposed, admired, and parented. Looking at the works, he felt a sense of having an audience, as if the men were excited to see him, reminding him of the first time he had wanted to show off to an older man. Two of his mother's boyfriends had separately complimented pubescent Zach for his great muscle tone and had performed unsolicited back massages. He had liked the feeling of being admired by these men and wanted to show them that, contrary to his mother's ego-shriveling insinuations, he did not have a small penis. He wondered if enjoying their admiration was what it was like to have a real father to whom he was bonded, an experience with which he was unfamiliar because his father had abandoned him in childhood. As a college student, he had been turned on by exhibitionism, such as at a game of strip poker when he had felt gratified by impressing his girlfriend and her roommate with his male body. But later this had morphed into a kind of compulsion, including male touching at the gym or sauna.

As he viewed the work further, Zach noticed that the contortions of the participants' feet during masturbation recalled how his mother's neediness, lack of self-esteem, and manipulative tendency had led to many imbalances in his life. Zach's mother had created a bizarre symbiosis with her son, whom she routinely asked to massage her feet with a pumice stone as he watched soap operas with her from the edge of the bed. After soaking her feet in a yellow plastic tub, he would use lotion to smooth her feet, every stroke reassuring to her that someone loved her. These sessions were frequently postponed by the presence of a lover, but when no man was in the house Zach absorbed the positive attention like a famished puppy. As a result, Zach not only got an education in how to reassure an insecure woman but also received a kind of apprenticeship in admiration for the male body, as he was forced to discuss in detail the positive aesthetic qualities of his mother's "man of the week." Yet, at the same time, the number of legs in the show reminded him of the large number of men who had walked through his mother's front door and then, a week or so later, back out, after, as Zach observed, making a small mess in his mother but a big mess in his life. Even so, some who were good-looking and muscular became models to which Zach could not only aspire but hope someday to possess. Thus the men whom his mother was trying to attract became substitutes for Zach's absent father, and instead of rebelling against his mother he assumed his best behavior in the hope of creating a normal family experience.

In the end, viewing *Self-Portraits* made Zach feel ambivalent, torn between celebrating what he began to see as his bisexuality and feeling judged, as his mother had shamed him during adolescence by commenting on "the sick things" he did in his room. But it also gave him a chance to work through these feelings by imagining a lineup of all his mother's boyfriends for him to inspect and grade, thus allowing him to revise scenes from his youth and adolescence to gain greater control over his memories.

The more Zach became aware of the psychology behind his responses to viewing *Self-Portraits,* the more he felt it had helped him heal old wounds. As a result, he gained an understanding that he no longer had to prove anything, observing: "I no longer feel pressure to prove to myself that I am a man, a beautiful person, and as worthy as any other human being. Feeling one of the group of men became a means to emotional healing from the days of being told by Mom I had a 'small dick' like my father. As I observe these artworks, I feel the empty core in my chest closing up, healing. I am effectively positioning myself at the level of their ankles and feet as a child to an adult, but my ingrained deference to elders no longer feels necessary as I begin to value my own opinions, ideas, and actions. How do I define myself from now on? I am my own man, not my mother's son or the forgotten spawn of a ghost dad."

Participating in *Self-Portraits* resulted in Zach's achieving a healthier approach to his sexuality through seeing that his need to be admired by men could ultimately be used positively to achieve stability in his life. This he could do, he realized, by living what he called a balanced bisexuality that better acknowledged his authentic self.

Another type of participatory function calls a viewer to exercise the mind or move the body or both, as a means of stretching themselves either literally or conceptually to try new things. This form offers a chance to work something out, as in role-playing with a therapist, only better since art cannot abandon you by going on vacation.

One work that can catalyze this type of participatory function is Anne Collier's *I Wish,* 2008.[2] In this work, the artist intentionally leaves a nearly blank lined sheet of paper, resembling a page torn out of a self-help book, for the viewer to fill in a wish, thereby prompting their self-expression and self-reflection. Entering the art to make a wish functions particularly well for an art seeker who requires concrete participation to gain insights.

This work helped one woman, Deb, learn to live more spontaneously and joyously. Despite many years of psychotherapy, during which she had mentally organized her life into columns of small things to avoid, Deb had never been able to maintain a broad perspective on her life. Collier's work prompted her to resist rigidly focusing on details to the exclusion of maintaining an overview perspective and developing self-expression. She was attracted to the work partly because she was addicted to self-help books, always adopting ideas of the latest self-help gurus rather than developing her own views, but *I Wish*, with its blank page, emphasized the significance of self-expression. Consequently, accepting the art's challenge to write her wish resulted in not just another failed exercise for self-improvement but a successful effort at self-healing. Instead of moving quickly onto the next self-help fad, Deb took the opportunity to examine her tendency to look outside herself to determine her life's direction instead of getting in touch with her inner self. As a result, she realized how looking to others had given her a false sense of her own identity and undermined her own self-expression.

In addition, the fact that the work's creator was a woman helped her gain useful insights about how her inability to connect with and rely on her authentic self had been initiated in her childhood. She recalled how her mother used to ask her to think for herself but all others in the family had dismissed her as an intellectual runt. As a result, Deb had nearly always deferred to elders in her life, lacking confidence to express ideas, which when she tried would sputter out like a trick birthday candle. So she had continuously rehashed old self-limiting thoughts and feelings instead of looking more deeply within herself for answers. This had kept her stuck or too focused on self-help fads. She now realized how her previous rationalizing and lack of connection had kept her in perpetual therapy, prohibiting her from fully developing her own identity and making goals in life based on it. After being prompted by *I Wish* to reflect more deeply, she characterized her current life as something she refused to categorize, thus liberating herself from self-limiting thoughts and opening a channel for discovery of her authentic self. Ultimately, the wish she wrote down while interacting with the work was to live more spontaneously, without fear of meaningful self-expression.

Another form of the participatory function involves movement within a defined space. Like when children play dress-up and temporarily become the people whose roles they are playing, movement within a work of art provides an opportunity to purposefully assume a different identity to discover insights about yourself.

For example, Christoph Buchel's *Dump*, 2008[3] encourages art seekers to enter the work to confront such issues as latent claustrophobia, having a cluttered inner life, and being wasteful, as well as to better appreciate how impoverished people around the globe live. To participate in *Dump*, an art seeker, Eden, donned the required shower cap and hard hat and entered a shanty house buried deep within a mountain of garbage containing such items as newspapers, a plastic hamper, Coke bottles, fruit boxes, lampshades, speakers, gloves, small appliances, plastic bags, a table, a bag of packing peanuts, mattresses, chairs, and even a sexy magazine.

Eden described the overall experience as follows:

Inside the mountain at the end of the ridged tunnel is a cramped living space, and an African man who speaks French but minimal English gives you a tour. Entering various rooms containing beds, tools, garbage in walls, dirt, made me feel I was in a subterranean shanty town. Apparently that's the point, to convey the experience of poor people around the globe. One small area containing mostly empty plastic PET bottles smelled so bad it made me want to gag. Everything was like a pigsty—tiny, cramped. I started to feel like a pack rat. One area opens up to a vertical ladder that is tough to negotiate but leads to another set of rooms emerging from a narrow hole. I walked into a garage with tools and a car up on a rafter and was told that someone sleeps there, and saw a mattress beneath the car. Finally, you enter into a large dining area like a lunchroom and are given the option to go back the way you came or to exit via a door, the latter option being the one any sane person would choose.

Her involvement in the work made Eden understand how wasteful her behavior had been in comparison with poorer, less fortunate people, and thus enabled her to better empathize with their plight. The artwork forced her to reflect on the dialectic of hoarding and discarding in her life on different levels. She realized how wasteful she habitually was with words, always needing to talk but saying very little except trivia, and how she tended to discard objects and people in relationships as if they were grease-stained paper plates. Further, she became aware of how emotional clutter robbed her of sleep and made her a hoarder, not of used diapers or newspapers but of negative emotions, that kept people at a distance, preventing intimacy and satisfying relationships.

Ultimately, the work made her more grateful for the opportunities she had in life, which she vowed not to squander in the future. She committed to being more conscious of how she hoarded and discarded things and, striving to avoid the negative aspects of these behaviors, decided this involved clearing both physical and emotional clutter from her life; training herself to live more efficiently; resisting the habit of talking about trivia; avoiding the tendency to throw away relationships without good reasons; recycling unpleasant experiences and making compost with them so they could grow more positive relationships; and inserting more "ventilation," or personal creative time, in her life to make her psychic domain more habitable.

Another form of the participatory function involves physically interacting with a work by touching or moving its parts. For example, viewers of Ted Julian Arnold's *Hope Chest*, 2008[4] are directed to "please touch" a freestanding marriage-themed sculpture combining paintings of faces and wedding attire on two wooden boxes, thereby rotating the cubes to combine any of four sides of the upper box with any of the four sides of the lower box to make potentially revealing combinations. For instance, the cubes can be positioned to show a man's face, a woman's face, or two color fields combined with a man's tuxedo, a bride's long-necked white dress with red flowers, a man's upside-down head wearing sunglasses and smoking a cigarette, or a woman's upside-down round face with red lipstick. Or the cubes might be positioned so they are not flush with each other, making it possible to view parts of even more combinations. In addition, hidden music boxes at the top of the work can be set in motion by an art seeker to hear various tunes that might resonate in different ways with the assortment of visual possibilities. One art seeker, Ron, who was habitually passive but struggling in his marriage because his wife was having a midlife crisis, alleviated his sense of powerlessness by touching the art to play with a variety of combinations. This allowed him to reflect on various aspects of his relationship, whether it was occasions involving passion, boredom, frustration, or resentment. Turning the cranks on the music boxes, and get-

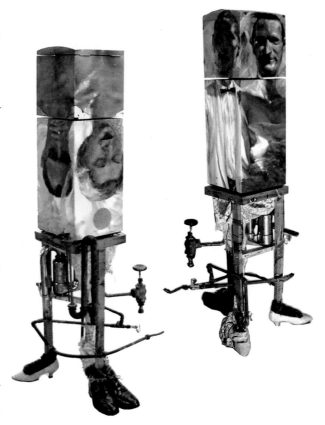

Hope Chest, 2008, Ted Julian Arnold

ting different tunes each time, such as "A Kiss Is but a Kiss," gave him an important insight about his current marriage problems. He realized that a marriage is not static and that it is a mistake to pretend people don't change. He saw that he needed to reevaluate his marriage based on this new perspective to see if his and his wife's acceptance of each other's transformations through time could be a way to reinvigorate their marriage. Participating in the artwork left Ron with a sense of the possibility of making his marriage work if he—inspired by the art's themes of transformation and variety—engaged in new experiences with his wife and remained flexible. Rotating the cubes to see new combinations and cranking out new tunes, he decided, had helped him let his obsessive thoughts about his wife go and initiate new approaches to his life with her so that they might once again make good music together as they had before their recent difficulties. This physical aspect of the artwork, here involving manipulation of parts, provides momentum for a viewer to enable positive action in life and repair a key relationship.

Perhaps the ultimate form of the participatory function is becoming art itself, which can also lead to personal insights, meditative practice, or increased creativity. A good example of how the participatory function works in this way is shown by how an art seeker, Carla, became involved with a piece of improvisational art by the artist collective Triiibe, a group consisting of Alicia, Kelly, and Sara Casilio, and photographer Cary Wolinsky, formed in 2006 to create political and social commentary enacted by museumgoers.[5] As Carla entered the gallery, she encountered two Triiibe members standing on wooden pedestals a few inches from the ground. On each of six other pedestals a placard had been placed with the title of an artwork to be completed through viewer participation, such as *Museumgoer*, 2008, or *Security Guard*, 2008, *Self-Portrait*, 2008, *iPod Addict*, 2008, *Best Friends*, 2008, *In Love*, 2008, *Man and Child*, 2008, *Sunday Afternoon at the Museum*, 2008, and *Portrait of a Balding Man*, 2008. The Triiibe members on the two pedestals modeled the kind of stillness that causes onlookers to do a double-take, like the unblinking human sculptures lining Barcelona's Las Ramblas, only without makeup and kitschy accoutrements. Carla recalled, "I was approached by a man with a large camera and asked if I would like to become an artwork." Normally very shy, Carla, who was with her boyfriend, first coyly insisted that she was too shy to participate but then decided to "go for it," no longer caring what other people thought. Carla was then invited to choose a placard with black lettering, resembling the informational placards to the sides of artworks on museum walls worldwide, and stand on the corresponding pedestal as a live human sculpture.

After choosing a placard on which was written *The Thinker*, 2008, she was instructed by the Triiibe members that she was to perform the concept her way and that it did not have to be like Rodin's *The Thinker*. They also gave her a trick of the trade—that by staring at a spot she could avoid distraction by onlookers. The final stage direction was the recommendation to "go inside." This helped Carla gain insight into her problem of chronic joylessness in her relationship. As she stood lost in concentration, she felt connected to and yet disconnected from her boyfriend, and as if she were feeling both serious and lighthearted. This made her reflect on the absence of fun in her relationship, wondering why her boyfriend disapproved of her staying out late with girlfriends and considered her fondness for her high-pressured job in corporate law a threat to their relationship. Carla then asked the art to guide her regarding the future of her relationship, realizing that the experience might reveal important information to help her make any decisions about sharing her life with him. Subsequently, she observed that he let his self-consciousness get in the way of focusing on his inner self, thereby confirming for Carla his lack of depth. As a result, she questioned why she wanted to live with someone who lacked flexibility and love of spontaneity. Instead, due to her experience in the *tableaux vivant* she realized that she wanted to participate fully in her life, unencumbered by such rigidity.

She described her experience in the following way: "I became what I intended—not just *The Thinker* but a thinker. The choice was fundamental to the ensuing experience." She could have chosen a role more in line with her usual activities, such as *Museumgoer*, 2008, but selecting something more personally challenging and following the instructions she'd been given allowed her to take advantage of a rare opportunity for self-reflection and thus gain more from the experience. Ironically, by standing still as art she discovered how her tendency to be constantly busy in activities was often at odds with the development of her creativity and an inner life. She then became aware of greater inner resources she could tap for creativity and more joyful life experiences.

Getting a handle on the various forms of the participatory function available to the art seeker helps pave the way to another, perhaps even more effective, means of insight, the permeability function.

4

Shocking Insight

THE PERMEABILITY FUNCTION

"I closed my eyes, and the sun burned crimson through the lids. I opened them and the Great Salt Lake was bleeding scarlet streaks. My sight was saturated by the color of red algae circulating in the heart of the lake, pumping into ruby currents—no they were veins and arteries sucking up the obscure sediments. My eyes became combustion chambers churning orbs of blood blazing by the light of the sun. . . . I was on a geologic fault that groaned within me." [1]

—Robert Smithson, above his *Spiral Jetty*, 1970

THE PERMEABILITY FUNCTION IS IN OPERATION WHEN ARTWORKS LOOSEN UP ART seekers, making them vulnerable so that core emotions and cognitions can be directly experienced. It is a way of undermining self-control to permit a path to the core of your being in the service of personal transformation. Once destructive behaviors and other "covering" emotions, which mental health professionals refer to as ego defenses, give way to awareness of painful truths down between the huge tectonic plates of the self, art seekers have a better chance of eventually being healed. In this function, art allows you to observe your primal emotions once your psychic fabric is teased apart so that you may weave that fabric back together in a way that transforms you for more positive experiences in the future.

Another way to look at this process is to see it as somewhat analogous to military basic training, with the permeability function substituting shock for sensory discomfort and emotional pain for physical interaction.

One art seeker, Gloria, was shocked into awareness of core issues and experienced the reopening of an old wound through the permeability function when she experienced a literally explosive work of contemporary art—Arcangelo Sassolino's *Afasia 1*, 2008,[2] art healing's answer to electroconvulsive therapy. In interacting with this work, in which an art seeker observes compressed nitrogen guns shooting green glass bottles at 600km per hour, explosions occur very quickly at unpredictable intervals, so loud they can be heard from anywhere within the building. The work's components include a stationary monster gun connected to imposing canisters of compressed gas, flying bottles, a back wall reminiscent of a metallic blackboard, and a mound of sharp glass shards on the ground—all contained within a long metallic cage reinforced by Plexiglas sides toward the back end where the bottles shatter, protecting viewers from physical harm. The fear generated by knowing something loud, dangerous, and frightening will happen but not knowing exactly when, is tremendous. Any comfort viewers may take from knowing this is occurring within a reinforced container is minimized by the realization that the noise comes from an automatic war machine.

For Gloria, the shock of *Afasia 1*, with its unstoppable violence of green glass crashing on the wall, initiated healing for dissociative amnesia in two ways: as a reminder of a past traumatic experience and as a reminder that, despite the chaotic action, the present was safe compared to her past traumatic events. The shock from the work triggered for Gloria memories of witnessing the near-drowning of her younger sister at a public pool while her self-interested father and distracted mother were not paying attention. At the time, Gloria was old enough to recognize something was amiss yet too young to do anything about it. The experience left her with a feeling of trauma combined with helplessness that, along with the negative impact of other traumatic childhood events, led to different forms of dissociation, including psychologically based amnesia of most memories prior to the age of ten.

While experiencing shocks due to the art, Gloria recalled one trauma after another, each of which, following the crash of a glass bottle, was demolished as if a psychic boil had been lanced by the permeability function activated by the artwork. In this way, she was able to heal not only the wound from having witnessed the near-drowning of her sister but also other old wounds—like the agony of covering up her mother's drinking when a friend threatened to come to her home; feelings of pain at her father's coldness when she attempted to rub his back for comfort; or having to hide from her father a paper bag with her mother's stolen cosmetics. After experiencing the work, which took place in a controlled setting, she became much more aware of how safe she currently was in her life.

In addition to being triggered by a sensory shock, the permeability function can also be initiated by visual shock. For example, Roger Ballen's *Head inside Shirt*, 2001,[3] a selenium-toned gelatin silver photographic print, shows an art seeker the illusion of headlessness, prompting reflection on the various meanings and implications of headlessness. In the image, a boy, whose position with his head in his tank top makes him appear like an otherwise normal human being but without a head, sits clutching a toy brontosaurus, next to an insect-like sculpture that is also headless. The fact that the boy looks alive but seems to lack a head gives the work a freaky, surrealistic quality, while the sculpture is reminiscent of a bug being crushed. At first the viewer experiences surprise and wonders how such an image is possible, before figuring out the cause of the illusion. For one art seeker, viewing the apparently headless boy, with the image's apparent references to human impairment, reduced her tolerance for unrelenting subtle ridicule by her coworkers and pressures from her family concerning fulfilling social obligations. The work brought her to an epiphanic realization that she had "no head," or no self, because of her deeply ingrained habit of allowing others to control her behavior. She saw

Him, 2001, Maurizio Cattelan

that unless she could start to clearly demarcate her boundaries and use her own mind to make decisions about how she wanted to live her life, she would "die" mentally and emotionally, unconnected to her authentic self. *Head inside Shirt*

forced her not only to consider her own negative habits and lack of consciousness but also more generally the nature of consciousness and being alive. Moreover, the artwork impressed on her the precariousness and fleetingness of life, further emphasizing her need to advocate for herself in order to live her life according to her own desires and dreams rather than those of others.

Another aspect of the permeability function involves an archetypal evil catalyzing a psychic shake-up that leads to personal insights. For example, one art seeker, a conflicted community leader named Grace, was forced to reassess her self-righteousness when viewing the sculpture *Him*, 2001[4] by Maurizio Cattelan. In this work, there appears to be a young boy on his knees, wearing a tweed coat. To get a look at his face, Grace had to walk up to it and peer at it closely, at which point she realized with a sudden sense of terror that this was not an innocent boy but Hitler. She felt as if she were staring the devil in the face and understood from the experience how evil can be insidiously cloaked by apparent goodness. This revelation prompted her to more objectively assess her habit of false moralizing, giving advice that often hurt others and which she did not even practice herself. The diminutive child-Hitler made her recall a recent encounter with a seven-year-old boy and his mother in a toy store, where she had self-righteously preached to the boy after he yelled to his mother as he pointed at a fun game, "There is a difference between what we want and what we need." Another revelation evoked by *Him* was her realization that she often attempted to ruthlessly manipulate others by making them emotionally dependent on her. Grace did this out of a selfish desire to feel needed, because she couldn't establish a feeling of security for herself in healthier ways. Perhaps the most insightful self-observation she had was that these habits stemmed from a deep, previously unacknowledged self-loathing.

The permeability function can also cut to the core of an art seeker's personal dilemma. Marina Abramovic's *Thomas Lips*, 1975–2008[5] helped one art seeker, Judy, with a chronically suicidal daughter gain a broader perspective so she could let go and live her own life. For a

Thomas Lips, 1975-2008, Marina Abramovic

long time Judy had been unable to empathize with her daughter's problems because of her daughter's repeated threats of suicide and need for reassurance from age fourteen on. The usual scenario was that she would pull back from her daughter; her daughter would do something horrible; then when her daughter did something that seemed ameliorative, such as taking better care of herself, Judy would reconnect with her again. The cycle would then begin anew when her daughter would sabotage her most recent small success and again threaten suicide. As Judy witnessed the artwork—consisting of a videotaped performance of the naked artist in a slow waking meditation whipping herself, eating a jar of honey with a spoon, drinking a bottle of wine, carving a star into her belly with a razor blade, then lying across a block of ice—the performance art broke through Judy's emotional defenses so she suddenly felt helplessness, fear, and guilt that she had carried for a long time tucked away in a private pocket of maternal failings. Judy endured great emotional pain recalling her daughter's years of suffering, able to finally empathize with her daughter by association as she empathized with the artist. Judy wondered to herself, "Is there any other work of art anywhere that screams 'Help me!' as loudly as this one does—seemingly in my daughter's voice?" After spending these agonizing moments with *Thomas Lips*, she could lift the safety bar from the amusement ride, dispense with burdensome guilt, and step far enough away from her daughter to stop adding fuel to her daughter's inflammatory behavior and live her own life again.

When the permeability function forces art seekers to confront emotional or behavioral problems, the only way out is by going through a revelation and healing process, much like experiences patients often have during therapy. Transformation can occur when there is a disruption and the disruption is integrated into the self, broadening perspective and increasing self-awareness. Such transformation is the focus of the transformative function of art healing.

5

Sorcerer's Sculpture

THE TRANSFORMATIVE FUNCTION

"Walk toward anything and it transforms. Metamorphoses always happen with proximity and distance. We do this with paintings almost without knowing it: we go to the Frick, there's a Vermeer of a woman in a fur collar, we get very close and we see no fur, we get farther off and we see fur. How can that be? It's ingenious. I thought a lot about things that transform as you get close. I also thought of why things transform to begin with—why we can see something within something."[1]
—Vik Muniz, Studio, Clinton Hill, Brooklyn, March 29, 1999

THE TRANSFORMATIVE FUNCTION OF ART HEALING CAPITALIZES ON CHANGE AS A theme in an artwork, leading to an art seeker's personal transformation. Change might appear in the art in any number of ways. It can be an obvious subject of the work or occur in a subtler manner, such as in its structure or materials; or it can be expressed through the depiction of movement itself or through the progression of time. This function focuses on arguably the most valuable aspect of any therapy: how it can catalyze positive change in many ways, whether by turning anxiety into contentment, interpersonal discord into loving understanding, shifting perspective, resolving a conflict, or otherwise effecting healing. The transformative function forces the viewer to relate to his own hidden traumas not obvious to others but nevertheless causing emotional distress and social isolation. The transformative function can be reassuring because every step, whether big or small, reinforces the belief that change is possible.

One type of change through the transformation function relates to reversal of stance from victim to victor. One art seeker, Jamie, who had endured past abusive situations, was able to transform herself from victim to victor by interacting with Fabien Giraud and Raphael Siboni's *The Abduction*, 2008,[2] a multilayered work of structural and thematic transformation. In creating *The Abduction*, the artists melted down a Native American bronze sculpture and made from it a brand-new work, promising to melt their sculpture down and re-create the original one after the exhibit. Thus the theme of transformation is reflected not only in the work's subject but also in its creation. Jamie considered the multiple levels, meanings, and types of transformation, including the seemingly traumatic events; the exploitation of creative labors in making the sculpture; the appropriation of art by a Native American, whose people have already suffered countless violations to their humanity and civil rights; the blending of cultural legends and eras; and finally, the imbuing of something dire—a rape, for example.

The original piece of art appropriated for transformation was a Southwest bronze sculpture created by Native American artist Ed Natiya entitled *Navajo Rollercoaster*, in which three children ride a fast-moving horse down a steep, jagged precipice, emphasizing the theme. The owner of the largest bronze foundry in Santa Fe, New Mexico, donated the work to the artists, who then took the bronze to a foundry out of the country to be melted down and recast to feature the same three figures but rendered differently, reflecting an ominous occurrence. In the recast sculpture, one child is located on top of the repositioned jagged slope with a hand outstretched to the sky, as if summoning aliens or entreating her parents, who might have left her behind, to retrieve her. Another child stands dazed,

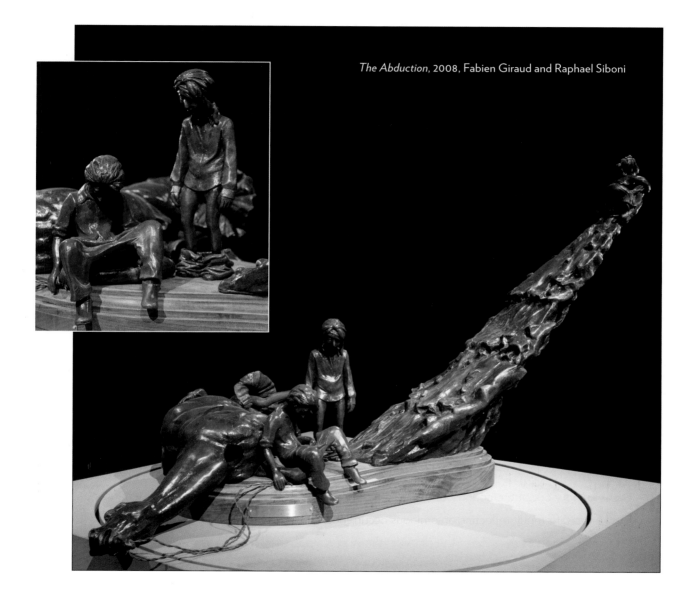

The Abduction, 2008, Fabien Giraud and Raphael Siboni

with his pants down around his ankles, while a third child sits with the dead horse's reins in one hand, inspecting his penis with the other. The horse has a huge long hole bored into it, so it is possible to see the face of one of the children at the other end. The work evokes sadness, confusion, and a creepy feeling that a violent event has occurred—like a partially recalled memory of sexual assault while under the influence of a surreptitiously administered date-rape drug.

Comprehending the types of transformation in the work, and understanding that since energy, including emotional and psychic energy, can be neither created nor destroyed and thus everything new is rooted in something old, allowed Jamie to achieve a new perspective on her past and present situation. She saw that the metamorphosis in *The Abduction*, from an atmosphere of innocence to one of sinister trauma—whether it occurs through the aggression of others or is the effect of cultural influence—paralleled her past metamorphosis at critical junctures. The work not only gave her new perspective on the past but also revealed new choices of reactions to former traumas since the children in the work model different reactions, from being shell-shocked, like the boy, to showing resilience, like the girl who stands on one foot with the other up in the air. Jamie understood that, interpreted differently, the little girl apparently summoning aliens or entreating her parents might also be summoning power from a spiritual source to effect a personal transformation.

Jamie gained strength for such a transformation from both the way the people in the work had been metamorphosed and the manner in which the artists had appropriated and changed the sculpture, as if alchemically. More importantly, Jamie realized that in the end she was responsible for recasting her own life by refashioning the same materials—her past pain—to create a more fulfilling existence as the artists had recast the sculpture to create a new artwork. After proclaiming, "I need to live!" Jamie was able to release her longstanding role as victim.

Ultimately, the work induced a kind of psychodrama soliloquy in Jamie's mind, emphasizing the transformation of roles from victim to victor:

What you did, the experiments you conducted on your young adoptee—the cigarette burns, the forcing me outside naked in front of the neighbors, the leash you threatened me with—will never leave. But I return all my suffering to you—I melt down and recast myself—the energy of ideas and events modified now.

Another type of change through the transformative function occurs through the control of chaos. Barton Rubenstein's *Ray of Light*, 2003,[3] inspired one art seeker, Antonio, to change himself on a fundamental physical level through meditative attention and communion with nature. The work is a sculpture with water coursing downward into the ground beneath a pile of small, smooth rocks built up in a mound around a stainless steel Japanese fan-shaped monolith. The viewer hears the water splashing, as well as the hollow sound made by the collection bin, unseen beneath the stones, from which the water is then pumped back up to be recycled. With its constantly flowing water, the work seems to symbolize an eternal river, recalling the well-known

Ray of Light, 2003, Barton Rubenstein

observation about change spoken by Heraclitus that, given the continuous flow of water in a river and passage of time, an individual can never step in the same river twice. The transformative experience is reflected not only in the flow of water but also in the colors changing with ambient light due to the reflection of passersby.

Ray of Light, in the way it exemplifies control of potentially chaotic nature, catalyzed a change in Antonio's behavior from that of a type A perfectionist taskmaster to a meditative spiritualist, allowing him to see ways to control the chaotic events of life more easily as well as to more calmly accept life's interruptions, even viewing them as desirable breaks from monotonous routines. For example, in the past spending money eating at an upscale restaurant with a date had invariably led Antonio to focus on some little negativity that then ruined an otherwise good meal, such as obsessing about a date's hardly noticeable flaw, like a skin blemish or slanted tooth. Now, however, he was able to tolerate even the tear in an oriental rug in his apartment, an imperfection cast intentionally by the rug maker to acknowledge that only Allah is perfect. This new level of tolerance was a testament to Antonio's resolve not to let the fact that he cannot control everything interfere with his contentment.

Another type of the transformative function involves change occurring by movement through time. One art seeker, Olivia, overcame stagnation and boredom in her life after viewing Reijo Kela's *365 Days—Reijo Kela's Video Diary of 1999*, 2006.[4] The video shows, with obvious humor, the artist gradually moving from the right to the left of a screen in approximately three-second scenes in each of which he performs a different action every day for a year, such as tumbling, bouncing, walking, climbing, swimming, running, dancing with arms flailing, twirling, skipping spastically, slipping, kicking his legs in the air, somersaulting, wearing clothes, wearing no clothes, holding a lit sparkler, walking through a sauna, walking with ski poles, in an art museum, in a bed convalescing from illness, with a vacuum cleaner, next to a buffet table, and wearing a Japanese *yukata* robe outdoors.

The work's use of changing activities and time's continuum as vehicles of transformation inspired Olivia to overcome stagnation and boredom in her life. She was able to do this by empathizing with the artist's generally positive attitude and rapid changes—the way he effectively danced through his life—even moving his legs while convalescing in bed. As a result, Olivia decided that in the future she would avoid stagnation and boredom in her life by keeping her interactions with difficult people to a minimum, including noxious family members, and ceasing to revisit the same ideas, places, pleasures, or disappointments. Instead, she would reserve her energy for more meaningful activities that would stimulate her curiosity and encourage her to move forward. She realized, "I need to make everyone else retreat into the background of my scenes to add color, to provide a foil, or a small narrative back-story for my emergence." She also recognized that, like the artist in the video, even while doing banal daily activities such as folding laundry, she could gain increased freedom through performing the tasks creatively or simultaneously reflecting on creative ideas. She vowed to remember the video in her mind's eye so she could recall in the future specific images that had inspired her new motivation to act positively, a process that involves the last function of art healing—the memory function.

6

Creating the Future by Way of the Past

THE MEMORY FUNCTION

"I would have spent my life trying to understand the function of remembering,
which is not the opposite of forgetting, but rather its lining.
We do not remember. We rewrite memory much as history is rewritten....
How does one remember thirst?"[1]
—Chris Marker, in *Sans Soleil*, 1983

THE MEMORY FUNCTION OF ART HEALING HELPS ART SEEKERS CONTINUE TO BENEFIT from their participation in the activity long after they exit the art museum or gallery. By offering possibilities for revising memory, providing hypothetical material for therapeutic role-playing, and allowing the art seeker to retrospectively reassess past transformations, the memory function can serve as a yardstick for measuring progress in healing. We have seen how memory as a concept is a necessary tool for the practice of art healing, as well as for any psychotherapeutic process. We have also explored how works of art, through different functions, might evoke memories in different forms to help individuals face core issues and discover paths to healing. The memory function, however, additionally aids art seekers in several ways: by allowing access to primal memories; by encouraging the conscious revision of memories to assist in role playing for healing, facilitated by the unreliability of memory as a means of reevaluating scenarios; and by permitting continued participation in artworks seen in the past, to provide ongoing support for future challenges. In using the memory function, it is not necessary to determine what really happened in the past so much as it is important to use past painful memories as a substrate for creating new ones that permit a broader, healthier perspective on life.

The memory function can help you reassess your earlier transformations through art healing at times when demoralizing events or recollections seem to inhibit imagination or forward movement. This can be facilitated by asking yourself, during your initial interaction with an artwork, what you can take away from it to guide your behavior or goals. Asking the art to provide answers to questions about personal issues perhaps can be compared to ancient Greeks seeking answers from the oracle at Delphi. And like the not entirely straightforward process of obtaining counsel from the oracle, art healing requires time and deep consideration for understanding the messages an artwork may offer for long-term benefits. Additionally, the memory function might be compared to retaining quotations of wisdom from an elder's speech for later recall when that wisdom is needed due to life's challenges. After interaction with artworks, an art seeker can use the memory function to recall past "visual quotations" from the works to conjure up aspects of them that support ongoing healing in the present.

To understand the memory function, we will examine art seekers' interactions with three types: using art to access primal memories, which occur while in the mother's womb; using art to consciously revise memories of the past to aid in establishing an emotional scaffold upon which to build a better future; and using art interacted with in the past for support during future challenging times.

An example of using art to access primal memories is the interaction of an art seeker named June with a work by Scandinavian artist Olof Nordal's *Cockeney*, 2005. June entered a dimly lit installation space and noticed five four-foot-diameter round pink bean-bag chairs—one that looked like a donut, another with a floral pattern resembling an umbilicus, another that looked like a curling, pointed tongue, another that seemed like buttocks, and others that looked like breasts with one or two nipples.

On the two back walls perpendicular to each other, June saw a close-up view of what at first seemed like the *Nova* episode "The Miracle of Life" with an endoscopic view of a fetus in its weightless amniotic environment. On the left screen, she saw breasts with nipples curving slightly like the ends of elf shoes. There was a small bit at the top of the breasts that could be either a small penis and testicles or a vulva and clitoris, ambiguous genital forms that seemed suggestive of a hermaphrodite. There were also what appeared to be elemental hands with clubbed fingers—four "fingers" on each hand with fingernails or perhaps toenails. On the other screen, she observed a big tongue and another hand with four digits, all parts of a multifaceted, organic dysmorphism. On a small white square shelf attached to one wall was a stack of square cards, which read:

Serpent, werewolf, scavenging beast
Monster in a woman's beard
My fantasy's progeny is released
A basilisk from a cock's egg reared

As she considered the possible meaning of the work, June interpreted the images as representations of a malformed creature. She also saw them as reflecting her maladaptation to life and inner neurosis, which was the cause of her inability to cope with stress, her drinking problem, and her difficulty with intimacy. Further, she viewed the message on the white card as being about a union between two beings that perhaps should never have mated, mirroring either her two irreconcilable personas or her past and present unsuccessful attempts to have fulfilling relationships. Yet at the same time, the work evoked in June memories of being in the womb, which she described as "a time when I was completely cared for, enveloped, floating. I am resolved to return to this state, somehow, despite the implications of the darker side to the place of comfort."

June's identification with an apparently mutant fetus or creature increased her awareness that something was wrong in her life and fostered a resolution to return to a healthier state of mind. Quoting the words of poet and musician Joy Harjo, June said, "I release you, fear! I release you!"[2] Using the memory function to gain awareness of the darker aspects of her life allowed June to better understand and release them so they would have no effect on her future behavior.

The memory function that involves consciously revising memories of the past to aid in establishing an emotional scaffold upon which to build a better future capitalizes on the unreliability of memory—the uncertainty of knowing precisely what happened in the past. Like eyewitnesses with divergent descriptions of the same event, we can never totally trust our memories. This aspect of the memory function can also be affected by the so-called last case bias in which most recent significant memories tend to supplant less important past memories, such as when an individual reads a book but revises the memory of its contents after seeing a movie based on the story. Not only can time be a factor in supplanting memories, but intensity of experience can as well, with the most intense memories supplanting the less intense ones. Regarding how memories are formed due to intensity of experience, Catherine Lupton says of Chris Marker's seminal work: "*La Jetee* recognizes that memories become memories 'on account of their scars'; their intensity is directly related to the proximity of trauma and loss, and the paradoxical function of memory is both to shield the subject from this trauma and to expose them to its presence."[3] An art seeker who permits art to supplant old memories can capitalize on this natural phenomenon to liberate the self from asphyxiating aspects of the past. Art can thus be a catalyst for reconfiguring perception through a conscious choice to forget as a means of making the future different from the past. The key to this aspect of the memory function is to permit the creation

Bicycle, 2001, Lori Nix

of fictitious memories and to relate to an artwork in such a way that fictitious memories can be valued as much as actual ones.

For example, Lori Nix's use of miniatures and dark humor in the works *Bicycle*, 2001, *Accidentally Kansas*, 1998, *Tent Revival*, 1999, *At Sea*, 2004,

Outpost, 2004, *Lovers Leap*, 2001, and *Elysium Fields*, 2001[4] readily allow an art seeker to remember and creatively revise events. *Bicycle* depicts a blue mountain bike with a streak of red along the seat on the ground, looking like it had been thrown down by a child who scampered away into the scraggly brush by the post and wire fence. A black sky looms overhead with a deep glow in back. Rather than eliciting a specific thought, the work evokes memories of intrigue, something sinister, or a state of uncertainty about knowing what exactly happened during an incident. While viewing this image, an art seeker named William was drawn by the humor into a realm of memory. He remembered being lost and disconnected from his mother and, after considering his own role as a parent, vowed to foster for his children a life emphasizing free play and discovery with a safety net of care and awareness of their whereabouts. Thus although the exact scene depicted by Nix might not have happened for the art seeker, it nonetheless provided a catalyst for the art seeker to bypass his own past and prevent repeating a pattern of neglect with his children.

Blimp, 1998, Lori Nix

Tent Revival, 1999, Lori Nix

Other works by Nix aid art seekers in creating partly fictitious past memories and using such blended memories for happier, more productive lives. For example, *Blimp*, in the Accidentally Kansas 1998 series, offered wisdom for shaping an art seeker's future. In the work, a blimp about to hit power lines evoked uncertainty about the potentiality of future danger, causing Sharon to interpret the work as a wake-up call to change a course of action before impending disaster. Similarly, Nix's *Tent Revival*, which shows colorful cars lined up outside a Southwest canyonlands white tent with worshippers and signs reading, "Jesus is coming" while the tent is being struck by purplish lightning portending future danger, caused Sharon to observe, "I see the creative potential in the darkness, and this is what keeps me interested and not so alone." Both these works helped her to revise past memories of an abusive boyfriend and to become aware of the necessity of altering her choices in life to avert pain and mistreatment in the future.

At Sea, which features ocean wave crests made from cotton and two life jackets without people, likewise expressed to Elaine an ominous message, yet the kitschy look of the diorama simultaneously added levity.

Outpost, 2004, Lori Nix

Elaine began to realize that she could use humor more frequently to heal wounds. Subsequently, in the future through activating the memory function, she would be able to maintain a more objective view on life that includes appreciating the potential humor of situations. She remembered an aunt that never seemed to take herself too seriously, and could assuage a skinned knee with a gentle smile and witty quip. Now, she would seek out a support system of friends who enjoyed using humor to get through difficult times.

At Sea, 2004, Lori Nix

Schoolbus, 1998, Lori Nix

Yet another work, *Outpost,* 2004, part of Lori Nix's Lost series, also aided an art seeker, Justin, to use the memory function. It depicts three Very Large Array radio telescopes positioned in different directions toward a partly cloudy sky that opens overhead to stars of different colors, with mountains on the horizon. In the darkness, one streetlight forms a cone of light on a woman hitchhiking, with the road so desolate that the possibility of anyone driving by seems almost as remote as the likelihood of the radio telescopes communicating with aliens living light years away. To Justin, this image represented a yearning for a connection that became clarified as a result of revising old memories of isolation as a child.

Viewing *Schoolbus* in the Accidentally Kansas series, which features a school bus abandoned in a valley of hills covered with spray-on snow, made art seeker Renée acutely aware of the need to abandon old childhood hurts. The artwork helped Renée supplant old painful memories with recent, more liberating ones to take a new road to the future.

Lovers Leap, 2001, Lori Nix

In addition, *Lovers Leap* helped Julia revise memories by capitalizing on the unreliability of memory. In the work, tiny figures jumping off a bridge to commit suicide seem cute even as they embody potential disaster. One in midair is already beyond a point of no return, although he might survive in the river below, while for the other still on the bridge there is yet hope. The ambiguity of motivation behind the actions of these figures allowed Julia to recall and revise a

Elysium Fields, 2001, Lori Nix

heart-wrenching past experience of being jilted by a lover. Unlike her memory of being distraught enough to be suicidal at the time, *Lover's Leap* made her realize in retrospect that she had not really been desperate enough to have jumped off a bridge. Through this realization, the memory of losing a lover became less intense, allowing her to heal the old wound and vow that in the future she would never let a failed relationship cause her to end her life—that her life was more valuable than any relationship.

Elysium Fields is another example of how a work can modify an art seeker's past sufficiently to create a more positive future. It features a barren expanse of ground with the silhouette of a Ferris wheel in the distance, backlit by the fading evening sky and two trucks with their headlights on. For an art seeker, perhaps the two trucks communicating with their headlights are like two parts of the self, or himself and another, against the backdrop of the barren landscape that evokes past emotional pain. The Ferris wheel represents joy that existed somewhere in the seemingly unreachable distance. The concept of resiliency—the ability of a person to survive against great odds—is distilled down to its essence in this image. And, as a result, memories of past harrowing experiences are supplanted by the newly acquired memory of a key survival mechanism.

The memory function is especially effective when capitalizing on an artwork whose main theme is the uncertainty of memory. For example, one art seeker attending Luke Stettner's exhibition *What Was, What Wasn't, What Will Never Be*, 2009, was drawn to a sculpture that focuses on a Plexiglas tube inside of which is a Radio Shack cassette recorder repeatedly playing the last words of the artist's father, who died when the artist was thirteen. The piece crystallizes the experience of loss so it can be absorbed in a new way. For the artist and art seeker, the Plexiglas display became a mausoleum, the tape player a coffin, and the audible whirring of the tape player's motor the perpetual sputtering of life in its final throes. While examining the piece, Jon discovered how more recently activated thoughts can supplant older memories, providing a means for healing. This occurred because the artist's tangible re-creation of his loss had therapeutic value for not only him but also, by extension, the art seeker since alteration and expression of the memory allowed a kind of control over the past. Upon hearing the tape, the art seeker empathized with the artist, whom he imagined improves his future by confronting and revising his painful past through the use of contemporary material. In the process, the art seeker's own memories of pain and loss could be recalled, revised, and healed by participating in the artist's recollection and revision.

Another work from Stettner's *What Was, What Wasn't, What Will Never Be* provides an additional example of remembering loss and revising and controlling it by reducing it to a physical form that can be transported. The work consists of three framed sheets of hand-pressed paper[5] displayed vertically in shadow boxes on the wall. The paper to the left has a light pink cotton candy color with the speckling and rough edges common to handmade paper; the paper in the center is white; and the paper to the right is light green. The faint words letter-pressed into the center of each sheet are, respectively: "What was," What wasn't," and "What will never be." These words correspond to the artist's source material for each—his father's possessions consisting of pink sales slips, handwritten notes on white paper, and canceled green checks. To an art seeker named Micah, the work recalled not only the memory of the artist's father but memories of his own father's struggle with business ventures to provide for his family, activities that had caused family stress and anxiety. Micah was able to use the artist's remembering, revising, and creating as inspiration for coming to terms with his own painful family experiences of the past so he could face the future less psychically oppressed by negative emotions.

Yet another work that helps in considering how the persistence of memory can be controlled by an artist and secondarily by an art seeker is Luke Stettner's *Close Your Eyes and Look Around*, 2009,[6] featuring a huge incandescent clear glass lightbulb suspended upside down on the wall, in front of a piece of paper with phosphorescent paint that reads, "Close your eyes and look around." This message glows in the dark, visible from outside through the windowpane, for about twenty minutes after the lights are turned off when the gallery closes for the night. When an art seeker stares at the bulb to try to make out the text in pale green ink behind the bulb then looks around the gallery, he can see the afterimage of coils repeated in all directions. This work evokes general notions of how remembering operates—what stays with you and what does not. Just like when looking at the lightbulb, an art seeker may initially not sense any way to escape from intense memories but, given a chance to turn away from them, they, like the glow of the afterimages, fade in intensity, freeing the art seeker for a more self-expressive and peaceful future.

A final important aspect of the memory function of art healing is the art seeker's use of works interacted with in the past as a yardstick to measure present progress in the healing of core issues that was initiated through art healing. As time goes by, it may be insightful to return periodically to artworks that particularly resonated with you if you can find them again and use them as markers to gauge your emotional and psychological evolution. This aspect of the memory function can be experienced, for example, by returning to works in permanent museum or private collections; works on the Internet; or works illustrated in magazines or books you might own or find in a library. By revisiting such works as you would an old friend weeks, months, or years after your original intimate interactions with them, you can assess from a greater perspective the healing that happened as a result of your creative participation. Although your experience of revisiting an artwork may not be as intense or revelatory as when you first encountered it, its ability to help you measure progress can be very gratifying.

afterword

Art healing remains a helpful means for me to continue to heal and gain important personal insights to improve my life in the future. Along with the other functions, I use the memory function to evaluate my progress in implementing the revelations I have received while art healing. When I now return to view Cornelia Parker's *Hanging Fire*,[1] I can see how far I have come since that stressful day when I impulsively dashed away from my family in anger and engaged in a serendipitous art healing session. Like the uneven pencil marks on the back of a growing child's bedroom door, my return to *Hanging Fire* gives clear indication of where I was then and where I am now. Encountering the work now, I look at it differently. I do not feel the need to glean all I can from it because I have done that already. And I feel my interaction with it is somehow more mature, like the deeper sense of connectedness one has with a partner of many years, without the need for all the emotional intensity of a relationship's infancy, adolescence, and midlife crisis.

It's not that I've grown weary from participating in art healing but that I have already done the fervent work of observing this piece of art, gleaning from it insights for healing, and I have allowed the insights I gained to persist in me. Now I can simply be present with the work, without an agenda, without a gaping wound, but with a contented feeling of accomplishment and gratitude. And I realize that even if I wanted to reexperience the intensity of my original art healing with *Hanging Fire*, I could not replicate it. This is vaguely akin to what might occur in cognitive behavioral therapy when one is exposed to an aversive stimulus long enough that it becomes familiar and, as such, incapable of triggering anxiety in the same way it once did. Or it is similar to the scientific understanding of how memory gets laid down by the brain as a process of long-term potentiation, where the brain's representation of objects, thoughts, or ideas, as they become increasingly familiar, no longer traverse a critical threshold required for neuronal depolarization.

I am also aware that overall my interactions with art have made me healthier than in the past when I faced core issues. If left to their own devices, the issues could have triggered some pathology and repeated cycles of painful memories had I not found a way out through the creative metaphorical mirrors and windows of art healing.

I hope that art healing will provide for you an enduring vantage point with which to view your life, as a window to peer out from or, alternatively, as a mirror held up to the nagging disequilibrium of the self. Or perhaps you may find art healing an inspirational means for gaining insight and shaking up your emotional status quo. Whether you engage in it to master trauma or simply as a guide to peaceful contemplation, may your art healing bring you pleasure, satisfaction, and understanding for a richer, more conscious life.

notes

PREFACE

1. AD REINHARDT, *Art As Art: The Selected Writings of Ad Reinhardt*, ed. Barbara Rose (Berkeley: University of California Press, 1991), 119.

INTRODUCTION

1. INGMAR BERGMAN, *Persona*, 1966, MGM Video, DVD release date February 10, 2004.

2. CORNELIA PARKER, *Hanging Fire (Suspected Arson)*, 1999, wire mesh, charcoal, wire, pins, nails, Institute of Contemporary Art, Boston.

3. ROBERT BLY, "The Long Bag We Drag Behind Us," *Meeting the Shadow: The Hidden Power of the Dark Side of Human Nature*, eds. Connie Zweig and Jeremiah Abrams (New York: G.P. Putnam's Sons, 1991).

4. A person addicted to heroin finds an effective treatment by the carefully controlled medical use of another form of opioid. Methadone, a medicine chemically related to heroin but considerably longer acting and unable to produce a high, occupies the brain's receptors, preventing withdrawal as well as the craving for dangerous fast-acting agents. Here, a distant cousin of a sought- after substance of abuse successfully treats an addiction.

5. CARL G. JUNG, *The Portable Jung*, ed. Joseph Campbell (New York: Penguin Books, 1984), 321.

6. **EDITH KRAMER**, "The Problem of Quality in Art," *Art Therapy in Theory and Practice*, eds. Elinor Ulman and Penny Dachinger (New York: Schocken Books, 1975), 52.

7. **NICK MAUSS**, "Abandoned Painting: Nick Mauss on Jochen Klein," *Artforum International* (October 2008), 359.

8. **PAUL J. SILVIA AND ELIZABETH M. BROWN**, "Anger, Disgust and the Negative Aesthetic Emotions: Expanding an Appraisal Model of Aesthetic Experience," *Psychology of Aesthetics, Creativity and the Arts* (2007) 1, no. 2, 100–106.

9. **UMBERTO ECO**, *History of Beauty*, tr. Alastair McEwen (New York: Rizzoli, 2005), 133.

10. **VALERIO CARRUBBA**, *Bird Rib*, 2007, oil on stainless steel, Museo d'Arte Contemporanea della Sicilia.

11. **ROY LICHTENSTEIN**, *Drowning Girl*, 1963, oil and synthetic polymer paint on canvas, Museum of Modern Art, New York.

12. **JOHN SZARKOWSKI**, *Mirrors and Windows: American Photography Since 1960* (New York: Museum of Modern Art, 1978), 19.

13. ⸻, 18.

14. **ANDREW NEWELL WYETH**, *Night Hauling*, 1944, tempera on masonite, Bowdoin College Museum of Art, Brunswick, Maine.

15. **DAVE MCKENZIE**, *Present Tense*, 2007, video, Institute of Contemporary Art, Boston.

16. **PHOEBE WASHBURN**, *While Enhancing a Diminishing Deep Down Thirst, the Juice Broke Loose (the Birth of a Soda Shop)*, 2008, Whitney Museum of American Art, New York.

17. **YESHE PARKS**, *Two by Two*, 2007, acrylic and collage on panel, Whitney Art Works, Portland, Maine.

18. **IRVING B. WEINER**, *Principles of Rorschach Interpretation* (Mahwah, NJ: Lawrence Erlbaum Associates, 2003), 8.

19. —————, 195.

20. PIERO GOLIA, *Manifest Destiny* (16-foot jump off the Tsien and Williams' ramp onto red polyurethane foam landing pad, three stunt mattresses), 2008, Site Santa Fe, Santa Fe, New Mexico.

21. KADER ATTIA, *Sleeping from Memory*, 2007, installation, Institute of Contemporary Art, Boston.

22. FRANZ WEST, *Mirror in a Cabin with Adaptives*, 1996, installation, Museum of Modern Art, New York.

23. NICHOLAS AND SHEILA PYE, *Sway—A Life of Errors*, 2006, performance art and chromogenic print. Angell Gallery, Toronto, Canada.

24. A phrase used by artist M. Ho, Pew Fellow in the Arts, 2005, in a talk given at the Tyler School of Art, January, 2006.

25. JASON RHOADES, *The Grand Machine/THEAREOLA*, 2002, mixed media, Whitney Museum of American Art, New York.

26. JEFF KOONS, *Puppy*, 1992, forty-three-foot (12.4 m)-tall topiary sculpture of a West Highland White Terrier puppy executed in a variety of flowers on a steel substructure.

27. JEFF KOONS, *Balloon Dog (Yellow)*, 1994–2000, high chromium stainless steel with transparent color coating, Steven and Alexandra Cohen Collection.

28. *Iconoclasts* on The Sundance Channel, original air date November 24, 2005.

29. Diego Velazquez, *Las Meninas*, 1656, oil on canvas, Museo del Prado, Madrid.

30. WALTER DE MARIA, *The Lightning Field*, 1977, earthwork, Dia Art Foundation, Quemado, New Mexico, and New York.

31. LEOPOLD BELLAK, *The T.A.T. and C.A.T. in Clinical Use* (New York: Grune and Stratton, 1971), 153.

32. MARK GREENWOLD, *All Joy Gone (For Marvin)*, 2000-01, oil on wood; *You Must Change Your Life*, 2001-02, oil on wood; *The Need to Understand*, 2002-03, oil on wood; *A Moment of True Feeling*, 2004-05, oil on wood; *The Excited Self*, 2005-06, oil on wood, D. C. Moore Gallery, New York.

33. Ling-Wen Tsai, *Rooftop—Sherman Street IV*, 2008, photograph, The Institute of Contemporary Art at Maine College of Art, Portland, Maine.

34. Ling-Wen Tsai, *Rooftop—High Street I*, 2008, photograph, The Institute of Contemporary Art at Maine College of Art, Portland, Maine.

CHAPTER ONE

1. Vincent Van Gogh, *Van Gogh: A Self-Portrait*, ed. W.H. Auden (Greenwich, CT: New York Graphic Society, 1961), 384.

2. Guenter A. Werner, *Ballet*, 2007, mixed media exhbition, Mike Weiss Gallery, New York.

3. Ernest Lawson, *Garden Landscape*, circa 1915, oil on canvas, Brooklyn Museum, Brooklyn, NY.

4. Willem Claesz Heda, *Still Life with Gilt Cup*, 1635, oil on panel, Rijksmuseum, Amsterdam, The Netherlands.

5. "Adriadne, the abandoned princess of Greek mythology..." from accompanying wall text of Giorgio de Chirico, *Piazza D'Italia (Italian Square)*, 1954, oil on canvas, Scott M. Black Collection, Portland Museum of Art, Portland, Maine.

6. Dennis Oppenheim, *Performance Piece*, 2000, steel, galvanized steel, epoxy, pigments, cement, bugles, fire brick, foam, and fiberglass, Johnson County Community College, Overland Park, Kansas.

7. Tim White-Sobieski, *New York Suite*, 2005, four–channel video, color, 6 minutes, 20 seconds, HD format, computer-coded animation loops, soundtrack by the artist, Space Other, Boston.

8. www.white-sobieski.com.

9. Lights in an artwork are presumed safe unless epilepsy prevents you from paying attention to flickering lights. Usually no one dies in the presence of art, but there are rare exceptions, like the tragic event involving Christo's umbrellas, which were carried by a rogue wind and killed someone.

10. KEN JACOBS, *Celestial Subway Lines/Salvaging Noise*, 2005, magic lantern projection, Anthology Film Archives, New York.

11. NICK CAVE, *Recent Soundsuits*, 2009, mixed media wearable sculptures, Jack Shainman Gallery, New York.

CHAPTER TWO

1. JEANNE SIEGEL, ed., *Art Talk: The Early '80s* (New York: Da Capo Press, 1988), 158.

2. A.C. GRAYLING, ed., *Philosophy 1: A Guide Through the Subject* (Oxford, England: Oxford University Press, 2000).

3. TAKASHI MURAKAMI, *Jellyfish Eyes*, 2001, lithograph, Kaikai Kiki, Tokyo, Japan.

4. HO, M., *Untitled*, 2005, collage, newspaper, Philadelphia, Pennsylvania.

5. MARC TRUJILLO, *1052 West Burbank Boulevard*, 2006, oil on canvas, Hackett-Freedman Gallery, San Francisco.

6. MASARU TATSUKI, *Decotora* 1998–2007 (Tokyo: Little More, 2007).

7. JENNY HOLZER, *BAR*, 2008, seven curved, double-sided LED signs, red and blue diodes on front, blue and white diodes on back, Cheim and Reid, New York.

8. PAWEL ALTHAMER, *Self-Portrait As a Business Man*, 2002-04, leather, textiles, plastic, glass, and paper, ICA Boston, and *Self-Portrait*, 1994, clothes, money, keys, bus ticket, passport and watch sealed in plastic, New Museum, Bowery, New York.

9. KELLY JO SHOWS, *Greed*, 2008, mixed media, Susan Maasch Fine Art, Portland, Maine.

10. Paul Kasmin Gallery, New York.

11. KENNY SCHARF, *Chocolate Donut in Space*, 2007, oil on linen, Paul Kasmin Gallery, New York.

12. JAMES HOWARD KUNSTLER, *Home from Nowhere: Remaking Our Everyday World for the 21ˢᵗ Century* (New York: Simon and Schuster, 1998).

13. PLATE 32 *Hover* series 1996–97, untitled gelatin silver prints, *Gregory Crewdson 1985–2005*, ed. Stephan Berg (Hannover, Germany: Hatje Cantz, 2005).

14. ANDREW LEONARD, *Idol*, 2007, multimedia installation, Bromfield Gallery, Boston.

15. Nicolas Clauss, *La Poupee*, June, 2005, http://www.flyingpuppet.com.

16. MARK GREENWOLD, *All Joy Gone (For Marvin)*, 2000-01, oil on wood; *A Moment of True Feeling*, 2004-05, oil on canvas; *The Risk of Existence*, 1997; *The Excited Self*, 2005-06, oil on canvas; *Why Not Say What Happened*, 2003-04; and *The Need to Understand*, 2002-03, oil on canvas; D.C. Moore Gallery, New York.

17. MARK GREENWOLD, *You Must Change Your Life*, 2001–02, oil on wood, D. C. Moore Gallery, New York.

CHAPTER THREE

1. JOHN WALSH, ed., *Bill Viola: The Passions* (Los Angeles: The J. Paul Getty Museum, 2003), 198.

2. ANNE COLLIER, *I Wish*, 2008, Xerox print, White Columns, New York.

3. CHRISTOPH BUCHEL, *Dump*, 2008, installation, Palais de Tokyo, Paris.

4. TED JULIAN ARNOLD, *Hope Chest*, 2008, mixed media, Susan Maasch Fine Art, Portland, Maine.

5. Triibe, a Boston-based performance art collective, consists of identical triplets Alicia, Kelly, and Sara Casilio and veteran *National Geographic* photographer Cary Wolinsky. On April 24, 2008, they "surprised" the new Boston Institute of Contemporary Art with a performance in which museum patrons were encouraged to become art.

CHAPTER FOUR

1. ELLEN H. JOHNSON, ed., *American Artists on Art: From 1940 to 1980* (New York: Harper and Row, 1982), 175.

2. ARCANGELO SASSOLINO, *Afasia 1*, 2008, installation, Palais de Tokyo, Paris.

3. ROGER BALLEN, *Head inside Shirt*, 2001, photograph, The New Museum, New York.

4. MAURIZIO CATTELAN, *Him*, 2001, sculpture, Centre Pompidou, Paris.

5. MARINA ABRAMOVIC, *Thomas Lips*, 1975–2008, video of performance at Guggenheim Museum, New York, viewed at Centre Pompidou, Paris.

CHAPTER FIVE

1. JUDITH OLCH RICHARDS, ed., *Inside the Studio: Two Decades of Talks with Artists in New York* (New York: Independent Curators International, 2004), 231.

2. FABIEN GIRAUD AND RAPHAEL SIBONI, *The Abduction*, 2008, bronze, color photograph, SITE Santa Fe Commission, Santa Fe, New Mexico.

3. BARTON RUBENSTEIN, *Ray of Light*, 2003, stainless steel, Shidoni Foundry, Tesuque, New Mexico.

4. REIJO KELA, *365 Days—Reijo Kela's Video Diary of 1999*, 2006, video 18 minutes, P.S.1, Long Island City, New York.

CHAPTER SIX

1. CHRIS MARKER, *Sans Soleil*, 1983, *La Jetee/Sans Soleil* Criterion Collection DVD, 2007.

2. JOY HARJO, "Poetic Justice," *Letter from the End of the Twentieth Century*, 1997, Compact Disc, Mekko Productions.

3. **Catherine Lupton**, *Chris Marker: Memories of the Future*. London: Reaktion Books, 2005.

4. **Lori Nix**, *Bicycle*, 2001, *Blimp*, 1998, *Tent Revival*, 1999, *At Sea*, 2004, *Outpost*, 2004, *Lovers Leap*, 2001, *Elysium Fields*, 2001, photographs, Miller Brown Gallery, Boston.

5. **Luke Stettner**, *What Was, What Wasn't, What Will Never Be*, 2009, handmade paper, three frames, Kate Werble Gallery, New York.

6. **Luke Stettner**, *Close Your Eyes and Look Around*, 2009, lightbulb, socket, wood, paper, phosphorescent paint, and Pyrex, frame, bulb, Kate Werble Gallery, New York.

AFTERWORD

1. **Cornelia Parker**, *Hanging Fire (Suspected Arson)*, 1999, wire mesh, charcoal, wire, pins, nails, Institute of Contemporary Art, Boston.

bibliography

ABRAMOVIC, MARINA. *Artist Body*. Milan, Italy: Charta, 1998.

ARAKI, NOBUYOSHI. *Araki*. Koln, Germany: Taschen, 2007.

AUDEN, W. H., ed. *Van Gogh: A Self-Portrait*. Greenwich, CT: New York Graphic Society, 1961.

BELLAK, LEOPOLD. *The T.A.T. and C.A.T. in Clinical Use*. New York: Grune and Stratton, 1971.

BERG, STEPHAN, ed. *Gregory Crewdson 1985-2005*. Hannover, Germany: Hatje Cantz, 2005.

BERLINSKI, DAVID. *A Tour of the Calculus*. New York: Pantheon Books, 1995.

BLY, ROBERT. "The Long Bag We Drag Behind Us." In Connie Zweig and Jeremiah Abrams, eds. *Meeting the Shadow: The Hidden Power of the Dark Side of Human Nature*. New York: G.P. Putnam's Sons, 1991.

CAHN, STEVEN M., ed. *Classics of Western Philosophy: Sixth Edition*. Indianapolis, IN: Hackett Publishing Company, 2002.

CATHCART, THOMAS, AND DANIEL KLEIN. *Plato and a Platypus Walk into a Bar...Understanding Philosophy through Jokes*. New York: Harry N. Abrams, 2007.

DRUCKER, JOHANNA. *Sweet Dreams: Contemporary Art and Complicity*. Chicago: The University of Chicago Press, 2005.

ECO, UMBERTO. *History of Beauty*. New York: Rizzoli, 2005.

GRAYLING, A.C., ed. *Philosophy 1: A Guide Through the Subject*. Oxford, England: Oxford University Press, 2000.

HARJO, JOY. "Poetic Justice." *Letter from the End of the Twentieth Century*. Honolulu, Hawaii: Mekko Productions, 1997.

Ho, M. Lecture, Tyler School of Art, January 2006.

Hoffman, Roald. *The Same and Not the Same*. New York: Columbia University Press, 1995.

Iconoclasts on the Sundance Channel, original air date November 24, 2005.

Johnson, Ellen H., ed. *American Artists on Art: From 1940 to 1980*. New York: Harper and Row, 1982.

Jung, Carl G. in Joseph Campbell, ed. *The Portable Jung*. New York: Penguin Books, 1984.

Paul Kasmin Gallery. *Kenny Scharf: New Paintings and Carzy Roy-Al*. New York: Paul Kasmin Gallery, 2007.

Kramer, Edith. "The Problem of Quality in Art." In Elinor Ulman and Penny Dachinger, eds. *Art Therapy in Theory and Practice*. New York: Schocken Books, 1975.

Kunstler, James Howard. *Home from Nowhere: Remaking Our Everyday World for the 21st Century*. New York: Simon and Schuster, 1998.

Kuspit, Daniel. *The End of Art*. New York: Cambridge University Press, 2004.

Lupton, Catherine. *Chris Marker: Memories of the Future*. London: Reaktion Books, 2005.

Masaru, Tatsuki. *Decotora, 1998-2007*. Tokyo: Little More, 2007.

Mauss, Nick. "Abandoned Painting: Nick Mauss on Jochen Klein." In *Artforum International* 47, no. 2 (October 2008): 359.

Millis, Keith. "Making Meaning Brings Pleasure: The Influence of Titles on Aesthetic Experiences." In *Emotion* 1, no.3 (2001): 320-29.

Reinhardt, Ad in Barbara Rose, ed., *Art As Art: The Selected Writings of Ad Reinhardt*. Berkeley: University of California Press, 1991.

Richards, Judith Olch, ed. *Inside the Studio: Two Decades of Talks with Artists in New York*. New York: Independent Curators International, 2004.

Samson Projects. *Gabriel Martinez: Self-Portraits*. Boston: Samson Projects, 2007.

SIEGEL, JEANNE, ed. *Art Talk: The Early '80s*. New York: Da Capo Press, 1988.

SILVERSTEIN, SHEL. *The Giving Tree*. New York: HarperCollins, 1964.

SILVIA, PAUL J., AND ELIZABETH M. BROWN. "Anger, Disgust and the Negative Aesthetic Emotions: Expanding an Appraisal Model of Aesthetic Experience." In *Psychology of Aesthetics, Creativity and the Arts* 1, no. 2 (2007): 100-06.

SIMPSON, BENNETT. *Philip-Lorca diCorcia*. Boston: Institute of Contemporary Art, 2007.

SZARKOWSKI, JOHN. *Mirrors and Windows: American Photography Since 1960*. New York: Museum of Modern Art, 1978.

WALSH, JOHN, ed. *Bill Viola: The Passions*. Los Angeles: The J. Paul Getty Museum, 2003.

WEINER, IRVING B. *Principles of Rorschach Interpretation*. Mahwah, NJ: Lawrence Erlbaum Associates, 2003.

artworks

MARINA ABRAMOVIC, *Thomas Lips*, 1975–2008, video. Viewed at Centre Pompidou, Paris.

PAWEL ALTHAMER, *Self-Portrait*, 1994, clothes, money, keys, bus ticket, passport and watch sealed in plastic. New Museum, Bowery, New York.

PAWEL ALTHAMER, *Self-Portrait As a Business Man*, 2002-04, leather, textiles, plastic, glass, and paper. Institute of Contemporary Art, Boston.

JANINE ANTONI, *Conduit*, 2009, copper sculpture with urine verdigris patina, framed digital c-print. Luhring Augustine, New York.

TED JULIAN ARNOLD, *Hope Chest*, 2008, mixed media. Susan Maasch Fine Art, Portland, Maine.

KADER ATTIA, *Sleeping from Memory*, 2007, installation. Institute of Contemporary Art, Boston.

ROGER BALLEN, *Head inside Shirt*, 2001, photograph. The New Museum, New York.

CHRISTOPH BUCHEL, *Dump*, 2008, installation. Palais de Tokyo, Paris.

MAURIZIO CATTELAN, *Him*, 2001, sculpture. Centre Pompidou, Paris.

NICK CAVE, *Recent Soundsuits*, 2009, mixed media wearable sculptures. Jack Shainman Gallery, New York.

NICOLAS CLAUSS, *La Poupee*, 2005, Web-based art. http://www.flyingpuppet.com.

ANNE COLLIER, *I Wish*, 2008, Xerox print. White Columns, New York.

GREGORY CREWDSON *Beneath the Roses* series, 2003-05, untitled digital C-prints, in *Gregory Crewdson 1985–2005*, ed. Stephan Berg. Ostfildern, Germany: Hatje Cantz, 2005.

GREGORY CREWDSON, *Hover* series, 1996–97, untitled gelatin silver prints, in *Gregory Crewdson 1985–2005*, ed. Stephan Berg. Ostfildern, Germany: Hatje Cantz, 2005.

GIORGIO DE CHIRICO, *Piazza D'Italia (Italian Square)*, 1954, oil on canvas. Scott M. Black Collection, Portland Museum of Art, Portland, Maine.

WALTER DE MARIA, *The Lightning Field*, 1977, earthwork. Dia Art Foundation, Quemado, New Mexico, and New York.

FABIEN GIRAUD AND RAPHAEL SIBONI, *The Abduction*, 2008, bronze, color photograph. SITE Santa Fe Commission, Santa Fe, New Mexico.

PIERO GOLIA, *Manifest Destiny*, 2008, 16-foot jump off the Tsien and Williams' ramp onto red polyurethane foam landing pad, three stunt mattresses. Site Santa Fe, Santa Fe, New Mexico.

MARK GREENWOLD, *All Joy Gone (For Marvin)*, 2000-01, oil on wood. D.C. Moore Gallery, New York.

MARK GREENWOLD, The *Excited Self*, 2005-06, oil on canvas. D.C. Moore Gallery, New York.

MARK GREENWOLD, *A Moment of True Feeling*, 2004-05, oil on canvas, D.C. Moore Gallery, New York.

MARK GREENWOLD, *The Need to Understand*, 2002-03, oil on canvas. D.C. Moore Gallery, New York.

MARK GREENWOLD, *The Risk of Existence*, 1997, oil on wood. D.C. Moore Gallery, New York.

MARK GREENWOLD, *You Must Change Your Life*, 2001-02, oil on canvas. D.C. Moore Gallery, New York.

WILLEM CLAESZ HEDA, *Still Life with Gilt Cup*, 1635, oil on panel. Rijksmuseum, Amsterdam, The Netherlands.

HO, M. *Untitled*, 2005, collage, newspaper. Private collection, Philadelphia, Pennsylvania.

JENNY HOLZER, *BAR*, 2008, seven curved, double-sided LED signs: red and blue diodes on front, blue and white diodes on back. Cheim and Reid, New York.

KEN JACOBS, *Celestial Subway Lines/Salvaging Noise*, 2005, magic lantern projection. Anthology Film Archives, New York.

REIJO KELA, *365 Days—Reijo Kela's Video Diary of 1999*, 2006, video. P.S. 1, Long Island City, New York.

JEFF KOONS, *Balloon Dog (Yellow)*, 1994–2000, high chromium stainless steel with transparent color coating. The Steven and Alexandra Cohen Collection, Stamford and Greenwich Connecticut.

JEFF KOONS, *Puppy*, 1992-95, forty-three-foot tall topiary sculpture of a West Highland White Terrier puppy executed in a variety of flowers on a steel substructure. Bilbao, Spain.

ERNEST LAWSON, *Garden Landscape*, circa 1915, oil on canvas. Brooklyn Museum, Brooklyn, New York.

ANDREW LEONARD, *Idol*, 2007, mixed media installation. Bromfield Gallery, Boston.

ROY LICHTENSTEIN, *Drowning Girl*, 1963, oil and synthetic polymer paint on canvas. Museum of Modern Art, New York.

ANDREA MANTEGNA, *Calvary*, 1457-60, wood. Musee du Louvre, Paris.

CHRIS MARKER, *Sans Soleil*, 1983, *La Jetee*, 1963, video. *La Jetee/Sans Soleil* Criterion Collection DVD, 2007.

GABRIEL MARTINEZ, *Self-Portraits of Heterosexual Men*, 2007, photographs. Samson Projects, Boston.

DAVE McKENZIE, *Present Tense*, 2007, video. Institute of Contemporary Art, Boston.

EDWARD MUNCH, *The Scream*, 1893, oil, tempera, and pastel on cardboard. National Gallery, Oslo, Norway.

TAKASHI MURAKAMI, *Jellyfish Eyes*, 2001, lithograph on paper. Kaikai Kiki, Tokyo, Japan.

LORI NIX, *At Sea*, 2004, photograph. Miller Block Gallery, Boston.

LORI NIX, *Bicycle*, 2001, photograph. Miller Block Gallery, Boston.

LORI NIX, *Blimp* from *Accidentally Kansas*, 1998, photograph. Miller Block Gallery, Boston.

LORI NIX, *Schoolbus* from *Accidentally Kansas*, 1998, photograph. Miller Block Gallery, Boston.

LORI NIX, *Elysium Fields*, 2001, photograph. Miller Block Gallery, Boston.

LORI NIX, *Lovers Leap*, 2001, photograph. Miller Block Gallery, Boston.

LORI NIX, *Outpost* from *Lost*, 2004, photograph. Miller Block Gallery, Boston.

LORI NIX, *Tent Revival*, 1999, photograph. Miller Block Gallery, Boston.

OLOF NORDAL, *Cockeney*, 2005, installation. Scandinavia House, New York.

DENNIS OPPENHEIM, *Performance Piece*, 2000, steel, galvanized steel, epoxy, pigments, cement, bugles, fire brick, foam, and fiberglass. Johnson County Community College, Overland Park, Kansas.

CORNELIA PARKER, *Hanging Fire (Suspected Arson)*, 1999, wire mesh, charcoal, wire, pins, nails. Institute of Contemporary Art, Boston.

YESHE PARKS, *Two by Two*, 2007, acrylic and collage on panel. Whitney Art Works, Portland, Maine.

PABLO PICASSO, *Head of a Woman*, 1962, executed by Paul Nesjar in 1971, cast concrete. The John B. Putnum, Jr. '45 Memorial Collection, Princeton University, Princeton, New Jersey.

NICHOLAS PYE AND SHEILA PYE, *Sway—A Life of Errors*, 2006, performance art and chromogenic print. Angell Gallery, Toronto, Canada.

JASON RHOADES, *The Grand Machine/THEAREOLA*, 2002, installation. Whitney Museum of American Art, New York.

BARTON RUBENSTEIN, *Ray of Light*, 2003, stainless steel. Shidoni Foundry, Tesuque, New Mexico.

ARCANGELO SASSOLINO, *Afasia 1*, 2008, installation. Palais de Tokyo, Paris.

KENNY SCHARF, *Chickendala*, 2007, oil and silkscreen ink on linen. Paul Kasmin Gallery, New York.

KENNY SCHARF, *Chips Galore aka Chip, Chip, Hooray! Aka Mother Chip aka Where the Chips May Fall aka Joy*, 2007, oil, acrylic and silkscreen ink on linen. Paul Kasmin Gallery, New York.

KENNY SCHARF, *Chocolate Donut in Space*, 2007, oil on linen. Paul Kasmin Gallery, New York.

KENNY SCHARF, *Cosmic Crude*, 2007, oil and acrylic on canvas. Paul Kasmin Gallery, New York.

KENNY SCHARF, *Great to Meet Shoe*, 2007, oil, acrylic, silkscreen ink and glitter on linen. Paul Kasmin Gallery, New York.

KENNY SCHARF, *Ketchup*, 2006, oil, acrylic, silkscreen ink and found objects (space vomit) on canvas. Paul Kasmin Gallery, New York.

KENNY SCHARF, *One Good Thing Leads to Another*, 2007, oil, acrylic and silkscreen ink on linen. Paul Kasmin Gallery, New York.

KENNY SCHARF, *Tang*, 2007, oil and glitter on canvas. Paul Kasmin Gallery, New York.

KELLY JO SHOWS, *Greed*, 2008, mixed media. Susan Maasch Fine Art, Portland, Maine.

Luke Stettner, *Close Your Eyes and Look Around*, 2009, lightbulb, socket, wood, paper, phosphorescent paint, and Pyrex, frame, bulb. Kate Werble Gallery, New York.

Luke Stettner, *Untitled*, 2007, Plexiglas, cassette recorder, endless loop cassette tape, and foam, large box, small box. Kate Werble Gallery, New York.

Luke Stettner, *What Was, What Wasn't, What Will Never Be*, 2009, handmade paper, three frames. Kate Werble Gallery, New York.

Masaru Tatsuki, *Decotora (Japanese Art Truck Scene)*, 1998-2007, photographs. Tai Gallery, Santa Fe, New Mexico.

Triiibe, Performance art (various), 2008. Institute of Contemporary Art, Boston.

Marc Trujillo, *1052 West Burbank Boulevard*, 2006, oil on canvas. Hackett-Freedman Gallery, San Francisco.

Ling-Wen Tsai, *Rooftop—High Street I*, 2008, photograph. The Institute of Contemporary Art at Maine College of Art, Portland Maine.

Ling-Wen Tsai, *Rooftop—Sherman Street IV*, 2008, photograph. The Institute of Contemporary Art at Maine College of Art, Portland, Maine.

Diego Velazquez, *Las Meninas*,1656, oil on canvas. Museo del Prado, Madrid, Spain.

Phoebe Washburn, *While Enhancing a Diminishing Deep Down Thirst, the Juice Broke Loose (the Birth of a Soda Shop)*, 2008, installation. Whitney Museum of American Art, New York.

Guenter A. Werner, *Ballet*, 2007, mixed media exhibition. Mike Weiss Gallery, New York.

Franz West, *Mirror in a Cabin with Adaptives*, 1996, installation. Museum of Modern Art, New York.

Tim White-Sobieski, *New York Suite*, 2005, four–channel video, color, 6 minutes, 20 seconds, HD format, computer-coded animation loops, soundtrack by the artist. Space Other, Boston.

about the author

Jeremy Spiegel, MD, is a psychiatrist in private practice and in public health in Portland, Maine, and New York City, and a diplomate of the American Board of Psychiatry and Neurology. His longtime fascination with the visual arts was launched while majoring in Art and Archaeology at Princeton University, where he went on to receive the Irma S. Seitz and Grace May Tilton prizes for his senior thesis, "Playing with Chance: Structure and Chaos in Twentieth-Century Art." He then attended Dartmouth Medical School, where he was issued the 1996 award for excellence in clinical psychiatry. As a resident in psychiatry at the University of New Mexico in Albuquerque, he presented a talk on how the writings Freud considered the most critical works of literature—Sophocles's *Oedipus Rex*, Fyodor Dostoevsky's *Brothers Karamazov*, and William Shakespeare's *Hamlet*—were relevant still, even in a general psychiatric clinic.

Dr. Spiegel appears frequently on "The Positive Mind" with Armand DiMele on radio WBAI 99.5 in New York City and blogs for *Psychology Today* magazine. He is also a regular presenter at the annual Creativity and Madness conference in Santa Fe, New Mexico. In addition to contributing articles to the general medical and psychiatric literature, he is the author of *The Mindful Medical Student: A Psychiatrist's Guide to Staying Who You Are While Becoming Who You Want to Be* (Dartmouth College Press, 2009), which received praise from the *Journal of the American Medical Association*.

For information on his lectures and art healing workshops, please visit www.thearthealing.com and www.seishinbooks.com.

order form

精神
SEISHIN
BOOKS

208 Vaughan Street
Portland, Maine 04102
phone: 207-772-3221
www.seishinbooks.com

QUANTITY   **AMOUNT**

_____ *Art Healing: Visual Art for Emotional Insight and Well-Being* ($19.95)   _____

Sales tax of 5% for Maine residents _____

Shipping and handling ($4.95 for first book; _____

$2.00 for each additional book) _____

Total Amount Enclosed _____

Quantity discounts available

METHOD OF PAYMENT:

❏ Check or money order enclosed

(made payable to Seishin Books in US funds only)

❏ MasterCard   ❏ VISA   ❏ American Express   ❏ Discover

Credit Card #:_____ Exp.:_____

Ship to (please print):

Name_____

Adress_____

City/State/Zip _____

Phone _____